Warman's Collec Firearms

FIELD GUIDE

James Card

Published by

Krause Publications, a division of F+W Media, Inc.
700 East State Street • Iola, WI 54990-0001
715-445-2214 • 888-457-2873

To order books or other products call toll-free 1-800-258-0929
or visit us online at www.krausebooks.com

On the Cover: Remington New Model Army revolver, .44 caliber, once owned by William F. "Buffalo Bill" Cody. Sold at auction: $239,000
Photo courtesy Heritage Auctions Co.

ISBN-13: 978-1-4402-3594-8
ISBN-10: 1-4402-3594-5

Designed by Jana Tappa
Edited by Paul Kennedy
Printed in China

Other Warman's Field Guides

Barbie Doll Field Guide

Bottles Field Guide

Depression Glass Field Guide

Hot Wheels Field Guide

M.I. Hummel Field Guide

Jewelry Field Guide

Tools Field Guide

U.S. Coins & Currency Field Guide

U.S. Stamps Field Guide

Watches Field Guide

Pre-War Factory Engraved Colt
Single Action Army Revolver

Introduction

Handguns

American Standard Tool ~ Ames ~ J.H. Dance & Bros. ~ Deringer ~ Hopkins & Allen ~ Krieghoff ~ Leech & Rigdon ~ Lindsay ~ Mauser ~ Merwin, Hulbert & Co. ~ James Reid ~ Savage ~ Sharps ~ Singer ~ Volcanic Arms ~ John Walch ~ Walther ~ Wesson & Harrington

Long Arms

Holland & Holland ~ Krieghoff ~ Marlin ~ Parker Bros. ~ Purdey ~ Savage ~ Sharps ~ Smith & Wesson ~ Spencer ~ Springfield ~ Thompson ~ Woodward

INTRODUCTION

Firearms Trigger Collector Interest

By James Card
Editor, Gun Digest the Magazine

Gun collecting has been going on since the first chunks of lead were fired out of old muskets but it wasn't until the Industrial Revolution that things got interesting. Early manufacturers and inventors changed the way firearms were produced and conceived and as a result, hundreds of makes and models of handguns, shotgun and rifles have been produced. Some of these guns have changed the world through their use in wars, exploration and hunting. Others were poorly designed from the start and fell by the wayside of history.

In between these great guns and junky guns are a lot of good guns that have great historical significance and have well-served generations of soldiers, hunters and law enforcement. If you are interested in finding and acquiring a collectible firearm, you have thousands from which to choose. Through personal tastes and interests, you will narrow the selections to something that is right for you.

Understanding Value

Like any collectible item, it is important to understand that the value of a used firearm greatly depends on its condition. Many people who have acquired old guns are naïve about gun value. They simply think that since a gun is old, it must be worth something. There are six grades of gun conditions and how a gun is graded is key to its value:

....

NEW IN BOX This means that the gun is in its original box with the papers that came with it. But this grade also means that the gun has never been fired and there is no sign whatsoever that the gun has been handled or used. This is the highest grade for a used gun.

....

EXCELLENT The gun may have been used but so gently and lightly that 98 percent of its finish remains as if it were brand new. All of its parts are still original and have not been swapped out with foreign ones. That includes no repairs or alternations.

....

VERY GOOD For this grade, all of the guns must be in good working order and 100 percent original but they may have had some minor repair work or alterations. The remaining finish should be around 92 percent.

....

GOOD Guns that fall in this value grade must have 80 percent of their original finish remaining. Alterations, repairs or additions are acceptable as long as they are not major ones. The firearm must safe to fire and in decent working condition.

**BROWNING SUPERPOSED
GRADE IV-W.410.**
Condition: Excellent.
$29,900

....

FAIR These guns are safe and in working order but only about 30 percent of their original finish remains. They may have had a major overhaul in a refinishing process or some other kind of alteration.

....

POOR These are pieces of junk that do not work and are unsafe to fire. They are rusty and any wood has cracked long ago. If you were to get this gun back into working order, it would require a skilled gunsmith putting in long hours and lots of cash. Unless the gun has some incredible historical significance, it is not worth your time or money to mess around with other than hanging it above a fireplace as a conversation piece.

The easy ones to figure out are New In Box and Poor. Anyone can tell the difference between an immaculate gun preserved still in its original gun case and a pitted gun rusted up so bad that it cannot function. The grades where people have problems and will argue about are the grades in between. It is important not to deceiver yourself about the gun's value in the grading system. Professional gun appraisers will notice small details that were missed in your amateur inspection. If you think the gun is in Very Good condition, it probably could be graded as only Good.

A Note about Gun Appraisers

If you think you have an old gun of value, or you are contemplating buying one, please do your homework. The landscape is pockmarked with unscrupulous people more than happy to separate you from your hard-earned money for something of dubious value. As always, knowledge is power. An excellent reference for antique American arms is *Flayderman's Guide to Antique American Firearms … and Their Values*. Norm Flayderman is arguably the world's best-known antique arms dealer and authority. Gun collectors and historians have long considered his book an indispensable tool.

Even with the help of a dependable reference such as Flayderman's, you may be well served getting the advice of a professional gun appraiser, especially if you think there is something unique or special about the gun you have or are considering buying. The appraiser will explain to you why the firearm is worth value X and why it is not worth value Y. Armed with that knowledge, you can make an intelligent buying or selling decision.

Scholar of the Gun

Many guns do not need to be appraised by a professional. There are so many guns out there of the exact same make and model that the differences in their value are negligible. Some of these guns fall into the category of "grandpa's old duck hunting gun." Many of these guns can be looked up in a price guide to gun values and you can get a ballpark figure of what it is worth. Two excellent resources are the *Standard Catalog of Firearms* and *The Blue Book of Gun Values*. Both offer an impressive depth and breadth of knowledge to the gun-collecting hobby.

If you think for some reason your gun is special, there is no reason why you cannot research everything there is to know about it and start forming an opinion of what the gun may be worth yourself, and here is something noteworthy about that: the value comes not from the gun but the journey of learning about it. The study of firearms involves lots of historical research and the understanding of gun mechanisms and manufacture. During your research you might learn about soldiers, cowboys, secret agents, hunters, titans of industry and great inventors and the impact they had not just on firearms but society and history as well.

The Guns of Heroes and Villains

Collectible guns receiving the most attention are ones used by both famous and infamous people alike. In the last decade, the guns of Theodore Roosevelt, Ernest Hemingway and baseball great Ted Williams have come up for sale with staggering results. For example, Roosevelt's specially made double-barreled shotgun set a world record when it sold for $862,500 at a James D. Julia Auction in 2010 while a Hemingway-owned Westley Richards side-by-side safari rifle sold for $340,000 at auction in 2011. Two pistols found on the bodies of famed Depression-era outlaws Bonnie Parker and Clyde Barrow after they were killed in 1934 sold for $504,000 at an RR Auction sale in 2012 (see page 226). In these rare cases provenance is everything, according to Wes Dillon, head of James D. Julia Rare Firearm & Military Division.

"The results (from the Roosevelt sale) were a direct reflection of the significance and importance of the man and his gun," Dillon said. Keep in mind, however, that these are exceptional, historical finds in the gun-collecting world and command extraordinary prices befitting the historical figure associated with the weapon. Some of these high prices are certainly driven by vanity – the desire to own a one-of-a-kind gun – while others are seen as investments. Either way, the right gun with the right history can realize staggering results at auction.

Collectible Guns as an Investment

On Internet message boards, there is considerable debate about collectible guns as an investment. There are arguments for and against the idea that acquiring guns could enhance your financial portfolio. It's true that certain collectible firearms have realized substantial return on investment. As with any investment, however, there is risk.

Here are some points to consider before you decide to include collectible firearms in your investment portfolio:

- Don't venture into gun collecting as an investment unless you know what you're doing.
- To get to the point of knowing could take years of study of both guns and the marketplace.
- If you decide to invest in firearms, it's often wise to choose a specialty, preferably with a type of gun that you are personally interested in. There are thousands of makes and models of guns, making it difficult to grasp market trends for each one. It's far better to get to know a few very well. There are numerous manufacturer-specific gun collector associations and they are a great place to start your research.
- Investing in anything—whether soybeans, vacant lots, weird artwork or old shotguns—entails a risk and usually one that you must ride out for a certain period of time until you see any type of return on your investment.

★★★★★★★★★★★★★★★★★★★★★★★

HANDGUNS

★★★★★★★★★★★★★★★★★★★★★★★

About 1,000 of these revolvers were manufactured from 1838-1940. Also known as the Texas Paterson, this revolver has great appeal to collectors because of its size (9-inch barrel), relatively heavy caliber and the association of the type with the Texas Ranger Jack Hays and verified use by military and civilians on the frontier. A Texas Paterson in outstanding condition is one of the great prizes of Colt collecting. This encased revolver, SN 515, .36 caliber, 5-shot cylinder with stagecoach holdup roll scene and shell-carved ivory grips, is such a prize. **$977,500**

Colt Paterson No. 5 "Texas" Model Percussion Revolver

$103,500

Rare Paterson revolver, SN 133, .36 caliber, with a 7-1/2" octagon barrel with tiny German silver front sight and the usual one-line barrel address "Patent Arms M'g. Co. Paterson, N.J.-Colt's Pt." with a snake and star pattern at each end. Only about 1,000 such guns were produced in the 1838-1840. The U.S. military ordered 150 of these revolvers, 100 of which were issued to the Pacific squadron in December 1841. In April 1839 the Republic of Texas purchased 180 of these revolvers for the Navy, which were later issued to the Texas Rangers. None of these military and state contract revolvers are known to ▶

have inspector marks. Given the time frame of these rare revolvers and the circumstances under which they were used, it is impressive that any have survived. Of those rare survivors few are in original configuration with any original finish. Only a small number of the original 1,000 revolvers had silver bands, as this one does. Muzzle and breech end of the barrel have two silver bands with two additional bands on bottom of barrel lug. Mounted with what is probably an original one-piece ivory grip constructed of two slabs of ivory attached to two spacer blocks in the middle. Barrel retains traces of thin original blue around front sight and in gullets of lug; frame is a smooth, even dark, brown patina. **$103,500**

PHOTO COURTESY JAMES D. JULIA, INC.

Cased Colt Model 5A Root Pocket Revolver

This percussion revolver, SN 2892, .31 caliber, has a 4-½" round barrel with two-line New York address. Blued finish. Case-hardened lever and hammer. Fluted cylinder. Spur trigger. Varnished walnut grip. Contained in an American walnut partitioned case. Original deep burgundy velvet lining with the following accessories: a key, steel cleaning rod with brass head; .31 caliber eagle and shield flask, spacer tool; two-cavity bowleg .31 caliber Colt's Patent bullet mold; 250 count blue label Eley Bros. cap tin with original mottled paper wrapper intact and lead ball supply. A superior cased example of this model revolver. **$28,750**

ELEY BROS Ld.
250
METAL LINED
CAPS.
Made expressly for
COLT'S Pt.
Belt and Pocket
PISTOLS,
Manufacturers, London.

HERITAGE AUCTIONS CO.

Colt Walker Model Revolver

Manufactured in 1847, with a total production of about 1,100, the Walker is the greatest prize of any Colt collection, according to *Flayderman's Guide to Antique American Firearms*. Slightly more than 10% of the original total manufactured survived to appear in modern day collections. The revolver weighs a massive 4 lbs. 9 oz. Serial numbering is in five companies, A, B, C, D, and E, beginning with the number 1 in each grouping. This Walker, SN D COMPANY NO 81, .44 caliber, has the usual configuration with 9" octagon to round barrel, brass front sight with fixed rear sight added in a dovetail at the cylinder end of the top flat. Top flat has a 1-line block letter left hand address "ADDRESS SAML. COLT, NEW-YORK CITY". Right side of barrel lug has a small "US" over "1847". The square back

brass trigger guard and steel backstrap contain a 1-pc walnut grip. Close examination of the barrel discloses that about 4-3/4" of the front portion is a replacement. The workmanship is first class but different coloration of the metal is still visible, with some variation in the rifling in the bore. The revolvers armed Dragoons of the U.S. Armed Forces engaged in the war with Mexico. They were issued to five different companies of Dragoons, A through E. Those revolvers which survived the War with Mexico in American hands remained in service well into the 1850s and in some cases even later, usually under adverse circumstances and are rarely found today in original configuration with any original finish. A large number of the 1,000 Walkers were destroyed when their cylinders burst and were replaced by different models of side arms. **$74,750**

Colt Walker Model Civilian Revolver

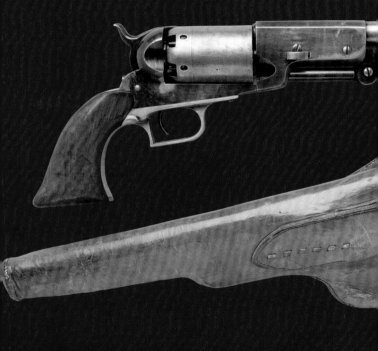

$690,000

About 100 Walkers, with serial numbers from 1001 through 1100, fell in the so-called "Civilian Range" and had no U.S. inspector markings but were otherwise like the military Walker pistols. This scarce model brings a premium among collectors. This example, SN 1078, known as "The Thumbprint Walker", is an exquisite example of the civilian revolvers manufactured at the same time as the commission from the U.S. Ordnance Department through the aegis of Capt. Samuel Hamilton Walker, in 1847. ▶

▶ This unusual revolver is in an exceptional state of preservation, and in rare full blue finish. The markings are extraordinary, sharp and perfect, with numbers matching throughout. The cylinder roll scene is sharp, with the easily visible cartouche markings: "Model U.S.M.R." and "Colt's Patent." Also readable is the marking of the engraver of the dies, Samuel Colt's friend and colleague: "W.L. Ormsby, Sc. N.Y." The slightly indented impression from the roll die at the rear section of the scene (by the cylinder stop cutouts) is pronounced. **$690,000**

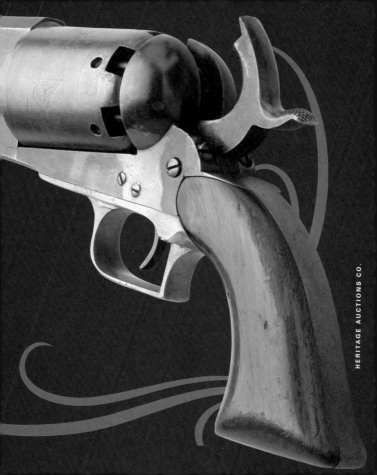

Colt Walker Model Revolver

Accompanied by a flask and holster, this very rare revolver, .44 caliber, is one of only 1,000 of these massive firearms produced for the U.S. Army in 1847. Prior to introduction of the Walker the only available repeating handgun was the Paterson revolver, which, although effective, was not terribly reliable and was prone to malfunction. The gun is named after Samuel Walker, a young Army captain who approached Samuel Colt looking for a more powerful handgun. This revolver has a 9" octagon to round barrel, German silver front sight and left hand one-line address. Right side of barrel lug is marked "1847". These pistols apparently saw service throughout the Civil War with very few surviving in original configuration with any original finish. Many of these pistols wound up in Mexico where they were generally altered by having their barrels cut.

$109,250

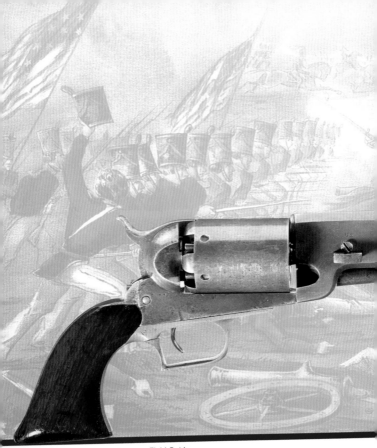

Colt Walker Model Revolver

This Colt Walker Model Revolver marked "B COMPANY No 163" was manufactured in 1847. This revolver was formerly part of the renowned William M. Locke collection, generally considered to be the finest grouping of American handguns ever assembled. Nearly all of the U.S. Contract Walker Model revolvers were used in the Mexican War or on the Texas frontier and saw hard service in the field. In 1984, Robert D. Whittington identified 150 surviving U.S. Walker Model Revolvers. **$86,250**

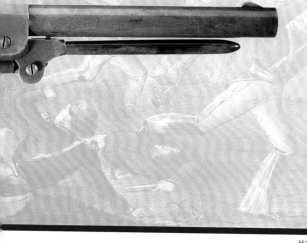

ROCK ISLAND AUCTION CO.

Cased Colt First Model Dragoon Revolver

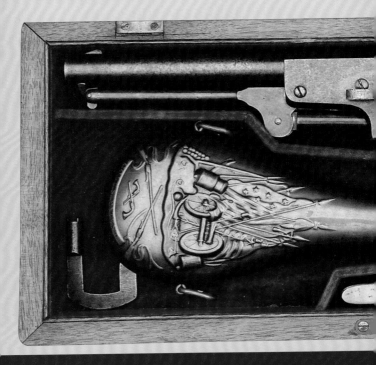

$181,125

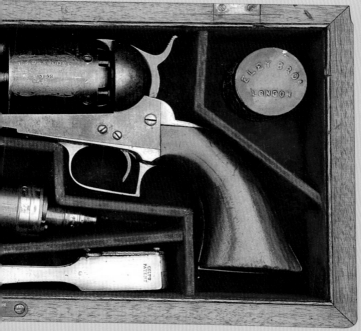

Only about 7,000 Colt First Model Dragoon Revolvers were manufactured from 1848 to 1850, according to *Flayderman's Guide to Antique American Firearms*. They are rarely found with any original finish and a cased revolver is extremely rare with only a few known. This revolver, SN 5842, .44 caliber, has been traced to C.H. Bowman, a member of the Tampico Rangers and a veteran of the Mexican War. The gun's provenance combined with its rarity, condition and extraordinarily rare case make it one of the finest examples known to exist. The 7-1/2" barrel retains 60-65% original blue mixed with flaked patina, strong blue in sheltered areas; rammer pivot retains about all of its original case colors turned a little dark; frame retains 30-40% faded case colors and the hammer dark case colors on left side and back edge with balance faded; cyl retains 75-80% strong but fading original blue and about 95% crisp, original Dragoon/Indian fight scene roll marking; The "U.S. DRAGOONS." and "COLT'S PATENT" legends are crisp with surrounding foliate patterns completely visible as is the Ormsby signature. Also accompanied by a pristine new "COLTS PATENT" powder flask with low mounted triangle hangers and plunger spout with "COLTS PATENT" markings on the ball cavity lid. **$181,125**

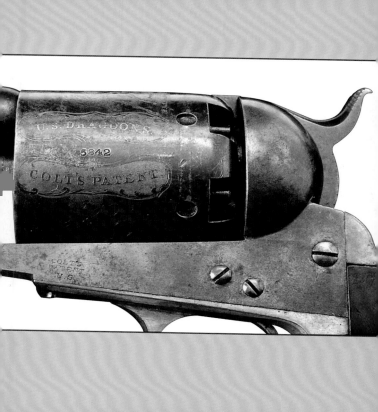

Cased Colt Baby Dragoon Pocket Model Revolver

The cased Baby Dragoon Model 1848 Pocket Revolver, SN 3035, is an extremely rare and much sought-after example. The revolver, .31 caliber, 5-shot cylinder, has a 5" octagon barrel with brass pin front sight with Texas Rangers and Comanche Indians roll scene. The grips of varnished walnut. Rare leather-covered wood case, lined in deep brown velvet. **$80,500**

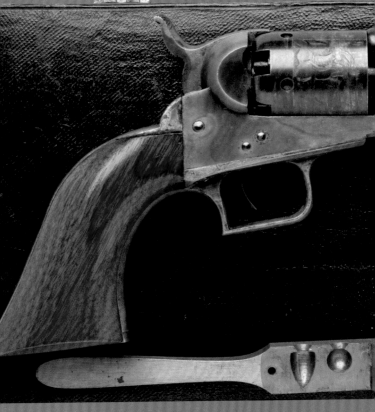

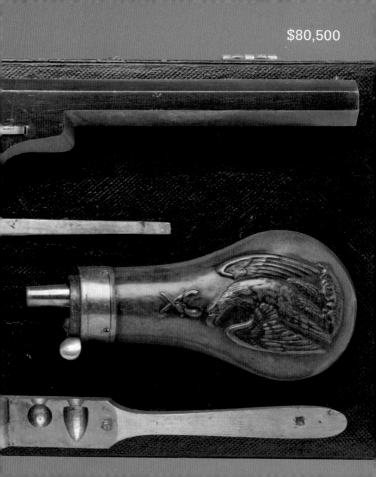
$80,500

Colt Baby Dragoon Revolver

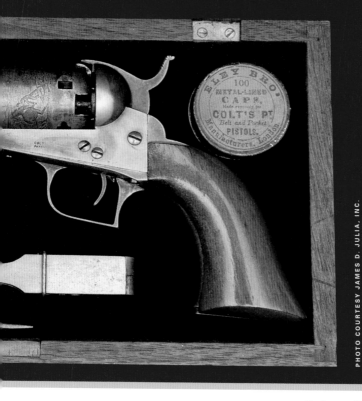

$31,635

The Colt Model 1848 was manufactured from 1847 through 1850, the first pocket model made at Colt's Hartford factory. About 15,000 were produced as a smaller version of the early .44 caliber Dragoon revolvers. The square-back trigger guard is a distinguishing feature. According to Colt's Pocket '49, only about 1,530 Baby Dragoons with rammers were produced and only an estimated 225 had the right-sided lever to rammer screw as is found on this revolver. This cased revolver, SN 11920, .31 caliber, is case hardened with 5" octagon barrel, brass pin front sight and 2-line New York City right hand address with dashes. Left side of frame has a tiny, centrally located "COLTS PATENT" and the silver plated square-back trigger guard and back strap contain a varnished 1-piece walnut grip with last three digits of the matching SN in back strap channel. Accompanied by its original Paterson style fluted lid walnut casing. Case is brown velvet lined with recesses in the bottom for the revolver cylinder, a wonderful double sided "COLTS PATENT", early eagle, pocket size flask, a brass 2-cavity "COLTS PATENT" bullet and ball Baby Dragoon bullet mold without sprue cutter, an L-shaped nipple wrench, a small lacquered tin of Eley's caps and a functioning key. **$31,635**

Colt London Third Model Dragoon Revolver

Manufactured from 1851 to 1861, a total of 10,500 Third Model Dragoon Revolvers were produced. The Third Model is the least scarce of all Colt Dragoons, and is the most representative type of Dragoon production, according to *Flayderman's Guide to Antique American Firearms*. Spotting a Third Model is relatively easy: look for the combination of rectangular cylinder stop slots and rounded trigger guard, the two basic features. This revolver, SN 129, .44 caliber, has a 7-1/2" octagon to round barrel, German silver front sight and engraved address "COL. COLT. LONDON." Left side of frame has "COLTS PATENT" engraved in a ribbon. The silver plated brass trigger guard and backstrap contain a burl walnut deluxe one-piece grip. **$29,900**

PHOTO COURTESY JAMES D. JULIA, INC.

Martially Marked Colt
Third Model Dragoon Revolver

This revolver, SN 14797, came from the Smithsonian Institution National Museum of American History collection, and had been traded for a Gatling Gun by the museum staff. (See the letter to the right) The Dragoon, .44 caliber, six-shot cylinder with Texas Rangers and Indians roll scene, has a 7-1/2" part round, part octagon barrel with brass blade front sight. Top flat of barrel lug stamped: Address Saml. Colt/New-York City within brackets. "Colts/Patent/U.S." on left side of frame. Blued, with color case-hardened frame, hammer, and loading lever. Plain brass gripstraps. The grips of varnished walnut. Left grip with inspector cartouche LCA, the right grip marked RHKW. Varnished mahogany case with brass-bound corners on lid, lined in burgundy velvet. Embossed stand of arms powder flask, blued steel double cavity bullet mold, tin of Eley Bros. percussion caps with embossed lid and paper label encircling can, as well as packet of Hazard Powder Co. waterproof cartridges. **$97,750**

AUG 2 8 1973

Air Mail

Mr. Al Cali
R. Cali & Bro.
20430 Stevens Creek Boulevard
Cupertino, California 95014

Dear Mr. Cali:

Your letter of May 25 to the Smithsonian Institution
pertaining to a Colt Dragoon Revolver in your possession
has come to me for reply. My apologies for this very tardy
answer.

According to our records, Colt Dragoon Model 1848 Revolver,
Catalog #222,399 was given to the Smithsonian Institution on
July 31, 1903 by the War Department and exchanged on April 21,
1958 with Mr. Arthur Sherman of Royal Oaks, Michigan. According to our catalog card, the cylinder was stamped with
Serial #16143, the frame was Serial #14797 and bearing
inspectors' stamps "LCA and "RHKW." None of these numbers
match the two remaining dragoon revolvers in our collections.
Although our records do not reflect precisely where these
pistols were prior to 1903. I was told many years ago by the
curator then in charge of the collections that it was among
a group of antique arms stored at Fort Monroe, Virginia.

Sincerely yours,

Craddock R. Goins, Jr.
Associate Curator
Division of Military History

Presentation Colt Third Model Dragoon Revolver

This historic, cased, Gustave Young-engraved Colt Dragoon, is a presentation revolver inscribed to "Colonel P.M. Milliken." Featuring ivory grips, the revolver, SN 16477, .44 caliber, six-shot cylinder with Texas Rangers and Comanche Indians roll scene, has a 7-1/2" part round, part octagon barrel with brass blade front sight. Top flat of barrel lug stamped "Address Saml. Colt/New-York City." As noted in "Colt Pistols" by R.L. Wilson and R.E. Hable, "Colonel Minor Milliken of the 1st Ohio Volunteer Cavalry was a brave and efficient officer in the Union Army, but was killed leading a saber charge against the Confederates at Stone River near Murfreesboro, Tennessee on December 31, 1862. Cited for gallantry by General Rosecrans, he was also noted in a report of Brigadier General John A. Wharton, C.S.A. – 'Colonel Milliken was killed by Private John Bowers, Co. K, Texas Rangers, in single combat.' Colonel Milliken left a widow and a four year old son, Paul M., who grew up to inherit his father's firearm. Condition indicates that the gun was not used in service but became a prized heirloom of the family. Paul became a colonel during the Spanish-American War, and well might have had his own name inscribed on the backstrap of the gun. He served as chief of police of Cincinnati from 1903-1911, saw more service in World War I and was successful in the insurance business until his death in 1934." **$805,000**

Presentation Colt Third
Model Dragoon Revolver

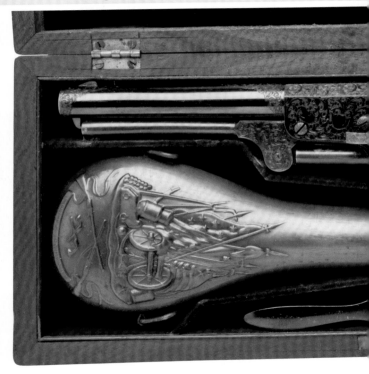

$805,000

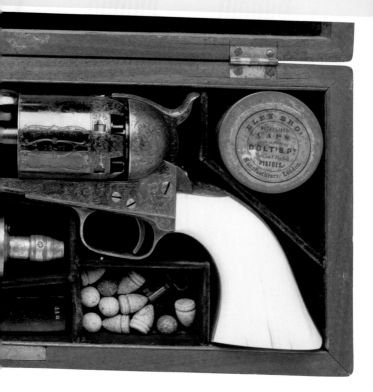

Colt Dragoon Revolver

Colt Factory Circular picturing Colt Dragoon Revolver, early 1850s. Measuring 10 3/4- x 16-1/2". $2,530

Presentation Colt Model 1849 Pocket Revolver

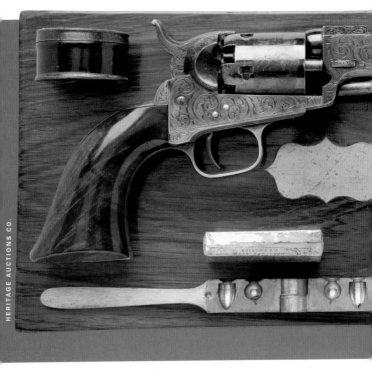

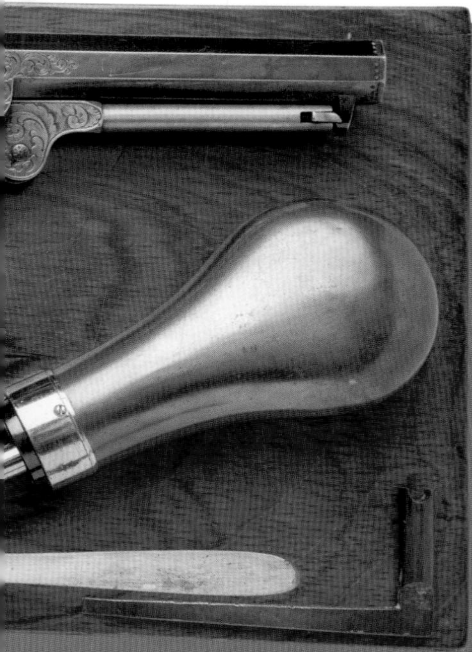

This deluxe-engraved Model 1849 Pocket Revolver, SN, 33598, was presented to gunsmith Anson Chase from inventor Col. Samuel Colt. Chase made prototype guns for Samuel Colt in the early 1930s. This presentation set honors the principal gunmaker who built the first of the Colt revolvers, and was a gift from the inventor himself. **$195,000**

Colt Model 1849 Pocket Percussion Revolver

This rare cased engraved Model 1849, SN 67771, .31 caliber, features 4" octagon barrel, brass pin front sight and hand engraved "Saml Colt" address. Revolver is engraved in donut style with full coverage foliate arabesque patterns on the frame, which extend over barrel lug and top side flats with matching patterns on rammer pivot. Cylinder is usual five-shot with stagecoach holdup scene roll marking and all five safety pins crisp and serviceable. Accompanied by fine brass bound mahogany case. **$28,750**

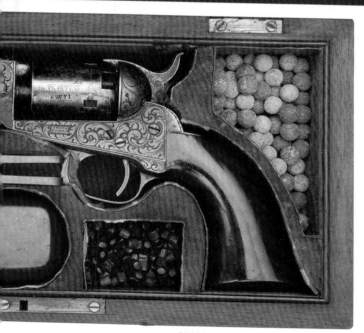

Colt Model 1849
Wells Fargo Revolver

Only about 4,000 of the so-called "Wells Fargo" model revolvers were manufactured; all without the loading lever. This revolver, SN 48234, .31 caliber, five-shot cylinder with stagecoach holdup roll scene, has a 3" octagon barrel with brass pin front sight. Top of barrel stamped ADDRESS SAML. COLT/NEW-YORK CITY. Left side of frame stamped COLTS/PATENT. Blued, with case-hardened frame and hammer, with silver-plated brass gripstraps. The grips are varnished walnut. **$29,900**

London Colt Model 1849 Pocket Revolver

More Model 1849 Pocket Revolvers were produced than any other Colt percussion firearm. Production began in 1850 and continued through 1873. The total of the Hartford-made series was about 340,000. The London Model 1849 shown here totaled about 11,000 from 1853-57. This was during the height of British colonialism throughout Asia, Africa and the Middle East. At that time British officers were required to provide their own sidearms with the Colt revolver being a favorite. This London model, SN 8364, .31 caliber, is blue and color case hardened with 5"

octagon barrel, brass pin front sight and two-line "ADDRESS. COL: COLT / LONDON" with long finial brackets. Frame has large "COLT'S PATENT" on left side and the large loop, silver plated, steel trigger guard and backstrap contain a highly figured light English walnut varnished one-piece grip with matching SN in backstrap channel. Cylinder is five-shot with stagecoach holdup scene roll marking and all five pins slightly battered but serviceable. Left side of barrel and cylinder have English proofs. Accompanied by its Colt London Agency mahogany casing. **$8,050**

PHOTO COURTESY JAMES D. JULIA, INC.

Colt Model 1851 London Navy Percussion Revolvers

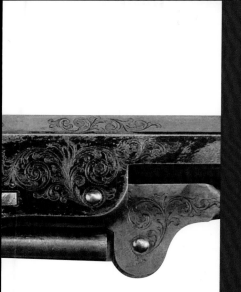

$80,500

The Model 1851 Navy Revolver was introduced in 1850 and manufactured through 1873. As one of the most popular of American antique arms, the Navy has come to be recognized as a collecting specialty of its own, according to *Flayderman's Guide to Antique American Firearms.* ▶

► This is a very rare case engraved pair, SN 23687 and 23647, .36 caliber, six-shot cylinder with 7-1/2" octagon barrels, brass pin front sights and one-line London addresses with arrows. Frames are identically engraved, probably by the same hand, with "Colts Patent" engraved in a ribbon on left side of frames. **$80,500**

Colt Model 1851 Navy Revolver, Martially Marked

The First Model attachable shoulder stock is the most rare of the Colt Model 1851 variations. Only a few examples are known, and none in the condition of this Martially Marked revolver with canteen insert. The revolver's Serial Number, 56806, appears on both revolver and on plain brass shoulder stock yoke mounting. The revolver has a 7-1/2" barrel blued and color case-hardened finish, with oil-finished walnut stocks. Left side of frame stamped "Colts/Patent." **$207,000**

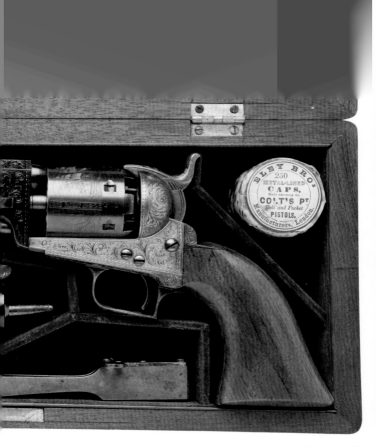

This fine and exceptional cased and engraved, Colt Model 1851, SN 2458, .36 caliber, six-shot cylinder with naval engagement roll scene, has a 7-1/2" octagon barrel with brass pin front sight. Top of barrel stamped: Address Saml. Colt New-York City. Scroll and border engraved barrel, loading lever, frame, hammer and gripstraps, in early open vine style. Left side of frame stamped "Colts/Patent." Blued, with color casehardened frame, hammer, and loading lever, with silver-plated brass gripstraps. The grips of varnished walnut. Varnished mahogany case. Embossed stand of arms powder flask, brass double cavity bullet mold with sprue cutter of bright steel, tin of Eley Bros. percussion caps with green paper label and in paper wrapper, blued L-shaped screwdriver/nipple wrench, key and miscellaneous percussion caps and extra parts. Shield-shaped brass keyplate inlaid on front of case. **$373,750**

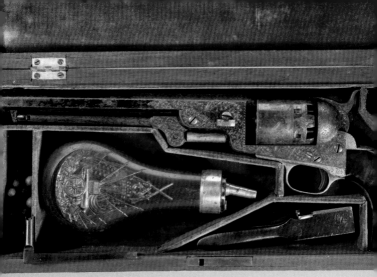

This cased Colt revolver embodies all the characteristics of an investment-grade collectable firearm: beauty, intrigue, rarity, desirability, and historical significances. Inventor Samuel Colt presented the gun himself to his friend, Capt. J.J. Comstock of the U.S. Mail Steamship Baltic. ▶

Col. Samuel Colt's Honeymoon Navy Revolver

$276,000

▶ The revolver tells a fascinating tale of America's first industrial tycoon, Colt, and his relationship with one of the 19th century's most noted navigators and sea captains, Joseph Jesse Comstock. By his 30s Captain Comstock had assumed command of some of the 19th century's most celebrated sailing vessels including the U.S. Massachusetts as well as the U.S. Steamship Baltic, for which this revolver is inscribed. The Baltic was launched on Feb. 5, 1850, and for its time was the most technologically advanced and most luxurious ship of its kind. It was onboard the S.S. Baltic that Colt crossed the Atlantic on his 1856 honeymoon with Elizabeth Hart Jarvis Colt. Colt's experience inspired him to have Gustave Young produce a pair of

exhibition quality revolvers reflecting the image of the Baltic and presented one to Comstock. The Baltic later played an important role in the Civil War, where it was used as a transport ship. In early 1861 President Lincoln gave future Assistant Secretary of the Navy Gustavus Fox a temporary appointment in the Navy and sent him with a small fleet led by the steamer Baltic to the relief of Fort Sumter. Fox could not relieve the fort before the Confederate bombardment forced its surrender. Major Robert Anderson announced the surrender of Fort Sumter aboard the Baltic. The back-strap of the revolver is inscribed: "Capt. J. J. Comstock. /U.S. Mail Steamship BALTIC. /From the Inventor". "From the Inventor" inscriptions are rare. **$276,000**

Colt Model 1851 London Navy Percussion Revolver

This Model 1851, SN 35232, .36-caliber, circa 1855, features a 7-1/2" octagon barrel, pin front sight and one-line address "COL. COLT. LONDON". Damascened steel trigger guard and backstrap contain a one-piece varnished walnut grip with matching SN in backstrap channel. Entire revolver including cylinder, rammer and handle, wedge, hammer, trigger guard and backstrap are beautifully damascened with intricate vines and flowerettes in heavy gold and a dark brownish metal background. Accompanied by an original English mahogany casing. This exact Colt is pictured on p. 141 in "Colt Engraving" by R. L. Wilson. **$34,500**

AID DE CAMP
GENERAL STAFF

Cased Pair Colt Model 1851 Navy Model Revolvers

This pair of Model 1851, SN 44284 and 44415, .36 caliber, six-shot cylinders with naval engagement roll scene, has 7-1/2" octagon barrels with brass pin front sights. Each revolver blued, with color case hardened frame, hammer and loading lever, and with blued steel gripstraps, with small triggerguards and short triggers. Varnished walnut grips. Each backstrap inscribed: "Aid De Camp General Staff" in block letters. $149,500

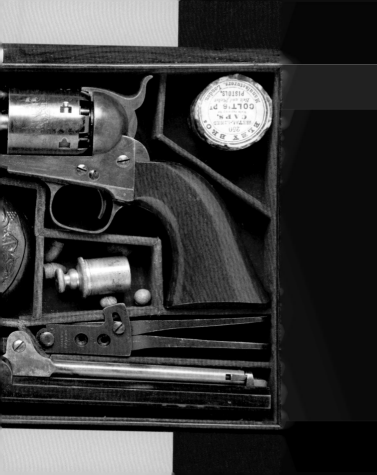

Custom Colt Model 1851 Navy and Model 1855 Pocket Sidehammer

$575,000

This impressive custom-made, cased, engraved set of guns was inscribed and presented to Loren Ballou, a trusted employee of Col. Samuel Colt. ▶

6 Combustible Envelope
CARTRIDGES,
MADE OF HAZARD'S POWDER
EXPRESSLY FOR
COL. COLT'S PATENT
REVOLVING-BELT PISTOL,
ADDRESS
COLT'S CARTRIDGE WORKS.

▶ The Model 1851 Navy revolver bears SN 37301 and is a London-made revolver. The backstrap bears the inscription, "L. Ballou/London." On the Model 1855 Sidehammer revolver, instead of a serial number marking, the name "L. Ballou" is stamped within the cartouche on the cylinder, and on the buttstrap. The Model 1851 has a case-hardened cylinder, as well as frame, hammer and loading lever, with the barrel browned, and the steel gripstraps plated in silver. The grips are varnished walnut, of a select, best quality grain and finish. The Model 1855 has an equally rare combination of a casehardened frame, loading lever and hammer, with blued cylinder and barrel. Beginning as early as 1851, Loren Ballou served as a trusted and well-placed employee with Col. Colt and his company in Hartford as well as in London. Ballou was a manufacturing engineer with Colt. **$575,000**

Colt Model 1855 Pocket Sidehammer Revolver

This fine and historic Colt Model 1855 Sidehammer with Charter Oak Grip was presented by Col. Samuel Colt to arms dealer J.I. Spies. The revolver, SN 5886, .28 caliber, five-shot cylinder with stagecoach holdup roll scene, has a 3-1/2" octagon barrel with brass pin front sight. The backstrap inscription documents the gift of this set to J.I. Spies. Engraved in Gustave Young style on the barrel, frame and hammer. The backstrap presentation inscription to Spies was executed in elegant script. **$345,000**

Colt Model 1855 Sidehammer Pocket Revolver

This cased and engraved Colt Model 1855 was presented by the company to the Rev. N.H. Gillett. Rev. Gillett served for nearly 20 years as minister of the Unity Presbyterian Church, Latrobe, Penn., until his death in 1868. Gillett's church was one of the oldest of that denomination in the United States. ▶

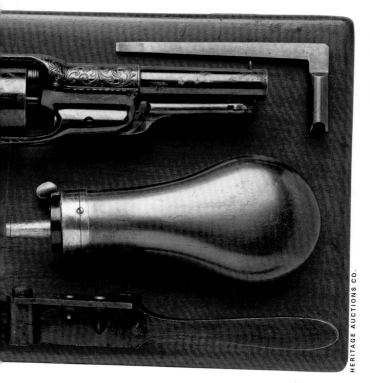

$92,000

▶ Gillett is believed to have been known to Gen. William B. Franklin, Colt's General Manager and Vice President from 1865 to 1888, and Richard W.H. Jarvis, Samuel Colt's brother-in-law, and president of the company from 1865 until 1901. The revolver, SN 11224 IE, .31 caliber, five-shot cylinder, has a 3 1/2" round barrel with brass pin front sight. Engraved in late vine style on the barrel, frame and hammer, the IE in the marking indicating "ivory, engraved." Conrad F. Ulrich engraved the revolver. **$92,000**

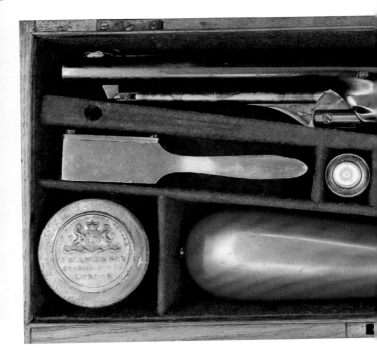

The Model 1860 was in produced from 1860 through 1873 with about 200,500 made. It was the major revolver in use by U.S. troops during the Civil War, with 127,156 of the Model 1860 Army acquired by the Union government for the war.

The successor to the Third Model Dragoon, the Model 1860 ranks third in total number produced of the various models of percussion Colt handguns, according to *Flayderman's Guide to Antique American Firearms*. This revolver, SN 154572, .44caliber, is blue and color case hardened with 8" round barrel, German silver front sight and 1-line New York U.S. America address. Left side of frame is marked "COLTS PATENT" and the left shoulder of trigger guard has the caliber marking. The blued steel trigger guard and back strap contain a 1-piece walnut grip with last four digits of SN in the buttstrap channel. Cylinder is rebated with usual 6-shots and Ormsby Naval Battle scene. Accompanied by an original English oak case. Bottom is compartmented for the revolver, a Dixon bag-shaped flask marked "COLT NAVY FLASK" on top of the collar, a blued steel "COLT'S PATENT" two-cavity bullet and ball mold with sprue cutter and marked on right side "44H", a large lacquered tin of Blanch and Son caps with brass label, a steel cleaning rod with wood handle, an L-shaped nipple wrench and a Dixon pewter oil bottle. There is also a functioning key. Revolver was manufactured and shipped to England at the height of Great Britain's Asian and African wars.
$57,500

Colt Model 1860
Given to Attorney General Bates

This Model 1860 Army Revolver, SN 11705, .44 caliber, was given to Attorney General Edward Bates, a member of President Lincoln's cabinet in November 1861, as part of a vigorous campaign by Samuel Colt to sell his revolvers to the Union Army for the looming Civil War.

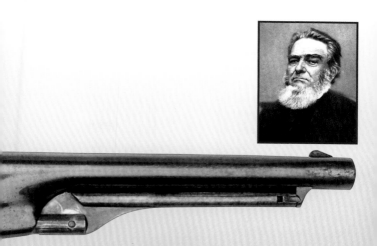

Colt presented 60 Colt revolvers to various high-ranking Army personnel and members of Lincoln's cabinet. Bates was a lawyer from Missouri, a strict Constitutionalist and apparently a very stern man, one who would probably have regarded an ostentatious gift as an attempted bribe. It is believed that Colt presented him with a single cased revolver without inscription instead of the cased inscribed pairs, which were part of this promotion. This revolver is standard configuration with 8" round barrel, German silver front sight, rebated six-shot cylinder with Ormsby naval battle scene. **$51,750**

Cased Colt Model 1860 Army Percussion Revolver

This rare Model 1860, SN 156656, .44 caliber, comes with canteen shoulder stock. The revolver is blue and color-case hardened with 8" round barrel, German silver front sight and one-line New-York U.S. America address. The three-screw frame, cut for shoulder stock, is marked with a small "COLTS PATENT" on left side and left shoulder of trigger guard is marked with caliber. Cylinder is usual six-shots rebated and has the Ormsby Naval Battle scene roll marking. The blued steel trigger guard and backstrap contain a varnished one-piece walnut grip. **$69,000**

Colt Model 1861
Navy Revolver

Manufactured from 1861 through 1873, about 38,843 Model 1861 revolvers were manufactured. A streamlined version of the Model 1851 Navy, the 1861 is one of the most attractive of all colt percussion handguns. This revolver, SN 19725, .36 caliber, is blue and color case hardened with 7-1/2" barrel, German silver front sight and 1-line New-York U.S. America address. The blued steel trigger guard and backstrap contain a varnished one-piece walnut grip. This revolver has extra polish finish which resulted in a lightened barrel address. Barrel and cylinder have small English proofs. Accompanied by an original English mahogany case. The 1861 generally saw extreme hard service throughout their working lives well into the 1870s before being supplanted by self-contained cartridge revolvers. Those sold on the English Market were usually purchased by military officers who used them continuously throughout the military campaigns in the far-flung British Empire. **$59,800**

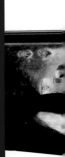

Historically Significant Colt 1861 Navy Percussion Revolvers

This rare engraved cased pair of Colt Model 1861 revolvers, SN 15147 and 15139, .36 caliber, are virtually identical with 7-1/2" round barrels, German silver front sights, slightly altered, with one-line New-York U.S. America addresses. The revolvers were presented to Charles Armory Clark, a Medal of Honor winner from the storied 6th Maine Volunteer Infantry. He earned the Medal of Honor for his action in the assault on Marye's Heights outside of Fredericksburg, Va., during the Civil War, and for his leadership in saving his regiment in the absence of his commanding officers by leading the regiment down a precipitous height at Banks' Ford, Va., while fighting off an entire brigade of Confederates. **$109,250**

Presentation Colt Model 1861
New Model Navy Revolver

$805,000

This exceptional, historic cased, engraved and presentation inscribed Colt Model 1861 New Model Navy Revolver is considered an icon within the arms collecting community. The revolver, SN 19928/E, .36 caliber, six-shot cylinder, was presented by the Colt Co. to E.W. Parsons, of Adams Express Co., Hartford, Conn. The E.W. Parsons Navy ranks among the finest and most historic of Colt percussion revolvers. It is a prime example of the appearance of a rare Colt set as it left the Colt factory destined for presentation. **$805,000**

Colt Model 1862 Police Revolver

The Model 1862 Police, made from 1861 through 1873, is considered by many collectors as the ultimate in streamlined design by Colt's factory in the percussion period. This revolver, SN 10679, .36 caliber, blue and color case hardened with 5-1/2" round barrel, has a brass pin front sight and one-line New-York U.S. America address. Silver plated brass trigger guard and backstrap contain a one-piece varnished walnut grip with last three digits of matching SN in the buttstrap channel.

Cylinder is usual fluted five shots. All five safety pins are crisp. These small revolvers were produced in limited quantities during the Civil War and became very popular with the military due to their small size but powerful caliber. After the war they continued in service on the American frontier, usually with little or no maintenance and are rarely found with high original finish. They remained in service well into the 1870s before being supplanted by the advent of the self-contained cartridge revolvers. **$18,400**

5 Combustible Envelope
CARTRIDGES,
MADE OF HAZARD'S POWDER
EXPRESSLY FOR
COL. COLT'S PATENT
NEW MODEL
REVOLVING
POLICE PISTOL.
36inch Calibre.
COLTS CARTRIDGE WORKS.

This cased Police Revolver, SN 40859, .36 caliber, five-shot semi-fluted and rebated cylinder, has a 6-1/2" round barrel with brass pin front sight. Blued, with casehardened frame, hammer, and loading lever, with silver-plated brass gripstraps. The grips of varnished walnut. Varnished mahogany case. **$32,200**

Colt Third Model "Thuer" Deringer

Made from 1870 through 1912, the Third Model, or Thuer Deringer outsold by nearly three times its No. 1 and No. 2 companions. This boxed pair, SN 4563 and 12739, .41- RF, nickel finish, 2-1/2" barrels, tiny half moon front sights, is marked "COLT" on the tops. Left sides of frames have the caliber marking. #4563 has tiny British proofs on bottom of barrel. Both are mounted with two-piece, smooth, birdhead pearl grips. Accompanied by an extremely rare two-piece, dark burgundy, cardboard box with pink top label. **$11,500**

PHOTO COURTESY JAMES D. JULIA, INC

Rare Colt Model 1871-72 Open-Top Prototype

This is a rare Colt Model 1871-72 Single Action Revolver prototype with an assembly number 3 only on the loading gate. The revolver, .44 centerfire, has a 7-½" barrel with New York U.S. America address and German silver front sight. Early pattern rifling. British proofs on the cylinder and left side of barrel lug. Blued finish. Brilliant case-hardened hammer, frame and loading gate. Navy-size gripstrap. Original one-piece ivory grips. Sold together with a 1985 letter from Greg Martin to a collector describing this gun and its collector origins. Finer than any known standard issue 1871-72 Open-Top .44. **$149,500**

Colt Single Action Army Revolver (Pinched Frame)

This rare revolver, SN 2., .45 Colt, is the second production Single Action Colt Army revolver made in the line of this famous model of which there were more than 250,000. It has rare pinched frame with nickel finish. Barrel has been reduced (from 7-1/2" to 5-1/2") and it has wonderfully carved raised ox-head, one-piece ivory grip with ruby eyes (one missing) and gold covered horns with a small oval plaque at the top of the right side inscribed "NO.2". Manufactured before mid-July 1873, this is one of the most rare and interesting of all the Single Action Army Revolvers. The revolver has seen hard service and is in "good" condition. **$63,250**

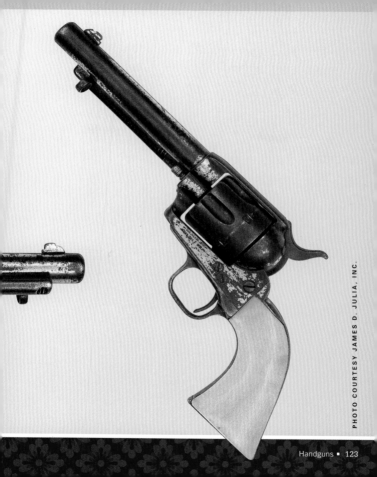

Colt Cavalry Single Action Army Revolver

This martially marked revolver, SN 19536, .45 Colt, has the usual configuration with 7-1/2" barrel, full front sight and one-line block letter address. Left side of frame has two-line patent dates and a tiny "U.S." Mounted with 1-piece walnut grip. Ejector rod housing is second type with bull's eye ejector rod head. The tiny "C" (A.P. Casey) inspector initials are found on barrel, trigger guard, top of back strap and cylinder. Casey-inspected Cavalry revolvers are scarce. They were inspected during December 1874 through March 1875. There was a total of 2,560 revolvers procured under those contracts and Casey and two others inspected them. Given the time frame that they were produced makes it almost a certainty that this revolver was among those issued to Cavalry units participating in the Indian wars. No original finish remains except traces of blue under ejector housing; revolver is an overall dark plum brown patina. **$7,475**

Rare Colt Rimfire
Single Action Army Revolver

Rare rimfire single-action revolver, SN 1144, .44 Henry, nickel finish with 7-1/2" barrel, full front sight and one-line block letter address. Mounted with one-piece walnut grip that has serial number in backstrap channel. According to *Flayderman's Guide to Antique American Firearms* there were about 1,800 of these revolvers produced from 1875-1880. These revolvers never gained strong acceptance on the American market. By the time they were produced centerfire cartridges were available in both revolvers and rifles which were far superior to the rimfire cartridges and could be reloaded easily. Colt sold the majority the .44 rimfire single actions to the Mexican and South and Central American markets. Those revolvers usually saw hard service, with little or no maintenance and largely had their barrels cut. It is rare to find any rimfire single action in original configuration with original finish. **$14,950**

Colt "Buntline Special"

Possibly one of the rarest Colt revolvers from a collector's standpoint, this Single Action Army Revolver is popularly known as the "Buntline Special". The revolver received its name after a dime novelist Ned Buntline – legend has it – gave five of these special long-barrel revolvers to famous Western frontier marshals: Wyatt Earp, Neal Brown, Charley Bassett, Bat Masterson, and Bill Tilghman at Dodge City, Kansas, around 1876. This is an extremely rare, totally original example of a Colt Single Action Army Revolver with 16" barrel, special front and rear sights and attachable factory stock. This revolver, SN 28886, is probably the best documented of the Buntline Specials. It comes with two Colt factory letters describing revolver as .45 caliber with 16" barrel and blue finish. ▶

$546,250

▶ A 28-page R.L. Wilson letter states "Serial No. 28826 is an excellent example of one of the most difficult and rare of all Legends of the American West firearms to acquire." In the letter Wilson also states this revolver serial number 28826 to be "one of the finest known." The revolver was featured on the January 1976 cover of "The American Rifleman." The revolver has a blue barrel, ejector housing, cylinder, trigger guard and back strap. The frame, hammer and loading gate are color case hardened. The one-piece walnut grip has a high polish varnish finish. The attachable stock is bronze with a nickel-plated finish and blued attachment knob. The revolver has a special extended hammer screw serving as a lug for the shoulder stock, a flat top strap with milled groove that is fitted with a unique, folding, long range rear sight and dovetail mounted front sight with nickel silver blade. **$546,250**

THE AMERICAN RIFLEMAN
JANUARY 1976

COLTS YOU SELDOM SEE

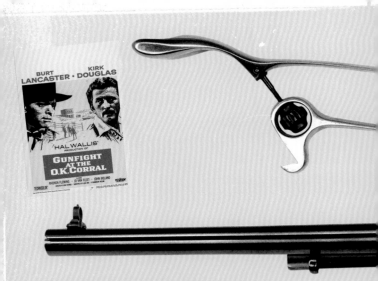

Colt "Buntline Special"

This Colt Single Action Army "Buntline Special", SN 28808, .44 WCF (44-40), features a 10" barrel and comes with a nickel-plated brass skeleton shoulder stock. Legend has it that Wyatt Earp found the long barrel handy in "buffaloing" or "pistol whipping" unruly characters in Tombstone, Arizona. It is also claimed that Wyatt Earp used a Buntline Special at the famous "Shootout at the O.K Corral," Oct. 26, 1881, in Tombstone. Condition: Very Fine. **$43,125**

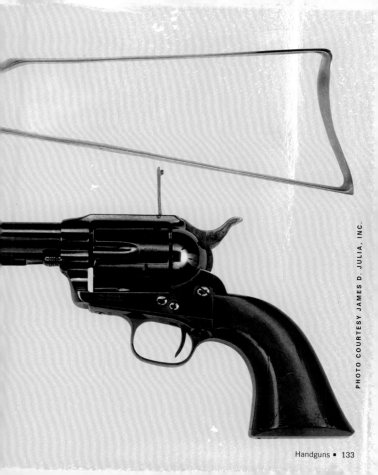

Very rare civilian/military cavalry single action army revolver, SN 41706, .45 Colt, blue and color case hardened with 7-1/2" barrel, full front sight and backwards or left hand 1-line block letter address. Very fine condition. Ejector rod housing is 2nd type with bull's eye ejector rod head. Left shoulder of trigger guard marked "45 CAL". Mounted with one-piece walnut grip. Left side of grip has an oval "DAL" (Capt. David A. Lyle) inspector cartouche under the date "1880". Right side of grip has a "DFC" (David F. Clark) sub-inspector cartouche. Letter from renowned Colt author and historian John Kopec authenticates revolver as completely original and one of very few known civilian/military revolvers. **$19,550**

Colt Civilian/Military Single Action Army Revolver

Nimschke Engraved Colt Single Action Army Revolver

$69,000

This Colt Army Revolver, SN 23641, .45 Colt, is beautifully engraved by renowned master engraver L.D. Nimschke with about B to A coverage of foliate arabesque patterns on frame and recoil shield with diamond and dot pattern on each side of barrel boss and hunter's stars on the sides of the base pin boss and ejector boss. Nickel and gold finish with 7-1/2" barrel, full front sight and one-line block letter address. Left side of frame has two-line patent dates and left shoulder of trigger guard is marked "45 CAL". Mounted with fine, smooth, Colt one-piece ivory grip. Ejector housing is 2nd type with bullseye ejector rod head. Cylinder, hammer and ejector housing originally gold washed over silver plating. Barrel, frame and grip frame are nickel plated. Top strap is engraved in circle and square patterns. Revolver appears to be unfired. **$69,000**

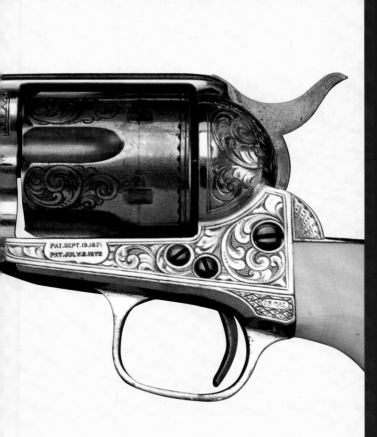

PAT.SEPT.19.1871
PAT.JULY.2.1872

Nimschke Engraved Colt Single Action Army Revolver

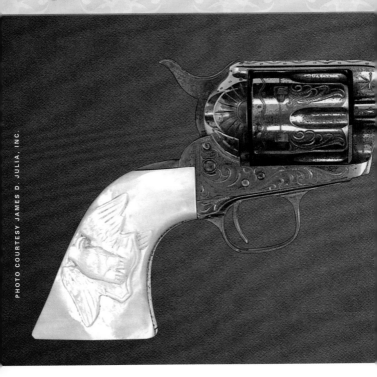

PHOTO COURTESY JAMES D. JULIA, INC.

Revolver, SN 105747, .45 Colt, nickel finish with 5-1/2" barrel, full front sight and two-line address. Left side of frame has three-line patent dates and caliber is marked on left front web of trigger guard. Mounted with two-piece pearl grips with a raised carved spread-winged eagle on right side. Revolver engraved in about "C" coverage by L.D. Nimschke with foliate arabesque patterns on sides of frame and snake and dot pattern over top strap. Recoil shield and loading gate are engraved in sunburst patterns with Hunter's stars on each side of the barrel boss. Base pin boss and ejector boss are engraved with snake and dot patterns. Accompanied by a Colt Factory Letter identifying revolver shipped to Hartley and Graham, New York, NY, on Aug. 21, 1884. Grips were apparently supplied by Hartley and Graham or a dealer **$25,875**

$25,875

Colt Cavalry Single Action Army Revolver

Martially marked revolver, SN 137537, .45 Colt, blue and color case hardened with 7-1/2" barrel, full front sight and 1-line block letter address. Very fine condition. Left side of frame has two-line three-patent dates and a small "U.S". Mounted with one-piece walnut grip that has last four digits of matching serial number in backstrap channel. Grip has a crisp "SEB" (Capt. Stanhope E. Blunt) cartouche on left side beneath the date "1891" and an "RAC" (Rinaldo A. Carr) sub-inspector cartouche on right side. Colt factory letter identifies revolver as being delivered to U.S. Government inspector at the Colt plant Jan. 20, 1891. Note: On military marked Colts, it is imperative that potential purchases be authenticated as many fakes have been discovered. **$23,000**

Dalton Gang Colt Single Action Army

The Dalton Gang is considered the last of the great frontier outlaw gangs that stalked the lawless American West. This Colt Single Action Army, SN 147307, was one of a pair outlaw Bob Dalton carried when he was killed during the ill-fated robbery of two banks in Coffeyville, Kan., Oct. 5, 1892. ▶

▶ The .45 caliber revolver has a 5-1/2" barrel, pearl grips and is engraved. Bob Dalton was ringleader of the Dalton Gang, who attempted to outdo crime sprees committed by the James Gang. Although known for making a living robbing trains, Dalton planned to rob two banks at once in broad daylight in Coffeyville. While the gang robbed the banks the townsfolk armed themselves for a shootout. The ensuing gunfight killed three citizens and Town Marshal Charles Connelly. Grat Dalton, Bob Dalton, Dick Broadwell and Bill Power were killed while Emmett Dalton was shot 23 times but survived. He was given a life sentence in the Kansas penitentiary in Lansing, Kan. He served 14 years before being pardoned. This revolver has an unparalleled amount of documentation for an outlaw gun. Colt firearms expert R.L. Wilson states "The documentation of serial number 147307 as one of the pair of Bob Dalton's Colt Single Actions carried on that fateful and historic day is in a classification of its own in the annals of firearms used by outlaws and lawmen in the Wild West." **$322,000**

Engraved Colt
Single Action
Army Revolver

Nimschke-style engraved revolver, SN 188022, .41 Colt, nickel finish with 4-3/4" barrel, full front sight and two-line address. Left side of frame has two-line three patent dates and Rampant Colt in circle. Mounted with modern replacement two-piece ivory grips with Colt silver medallions and lightly carved foliate arabesque patterns on heels. Revolver is engraved in L.D. Nimschke-style. Top strap is engraved in snake and dash patterns with foliate arabesque patterns extending over sides of barrel. **$5,750**

Texas History Colt
Single Action Army Revolver

This engraved SAA, SN 150668, .45, nickel finish with 4-3/4"
barrel, left side frame has two-line three-patent dates and
Rampant Colt in circle. Mounted with beautiful two-piece smooth
pearl grips numbered to revolver. Revolver is engraved by Cuno
Helfricht with about full coverage on frame consisting of foliate
arabesque patterns with punch dot background. Recoil shield and

loading gate are engraved in Helfricht's trademark sunburst patterns with snake and dot patterns on top strap. Colt Factory letter identifies this revolver as being shipped to J.C. Petmecky, Austin, Texas, on March 22, 1893, in a one-gun shipment. Petmecky was a gun maker and dealer in Austin whose shop was in business for more than 75 years supplying all manner of arms to local Texans, including revolvers to Texas Rangers, other lawmen, outlaws and many famous figures. **$97,750**

Colt Single Action Army Revolver Sheriff's Model

Made without ejector rod or ejector housing, the Colt SAA Sheriff's or Shopkeeper's Model was manufactured with a short barrel. This SAA, SN 122399, .45 Colt, nickel finish comes with a 4" barrel, full front sight, two-line address and cal marking on left side. Left side frame has three-line patent dates and Rampant Colt in circle. Mounted with Rampant Colt, eagle hard rubber grips. Colt Peacemaker Encyclopedia, speculates that there were fewer than 1,000 Sheriff's Model revolvers manufactured throughout the entire production and further reports that there are 10 known Sheriff's Model revolvers in the 122,000 serial range. Overall the revolver retains virtually all original factory nickel with only very minor nicks and scratches. Mechanics are crisp; brilliant shiny bore, probably unfired. **$57,500**

PHOTO COURTESY JAMES D. JULIA, INC.

Cased Colt Single Action Army Revolver London Model

These revolvers were manufactured to be sold through Colt's London Agency. This fine factory engraved revolver, SN 53371, with nickel finish, blued screws and 5-1/2" barrel, features full front sight and one-line Hartford/Pall Mall London address. Mounted with factory original one-piece pearl grip made with two slabs of pearl attached to wooden blocks to create the one-piece configuration. Engraving is in New York style by master engraver L.D. Nimschke or one of the craftsmen in his shop. **$32,200**

This "Rough Rider" U.S. Colt Artillery Single Action Revolver and holster, SN 116152, belonged to Colton Reed, a trooper in Company K in Teddy Roosevelt's Rough Riders. He is seen, standing, on the far left of the Company K photo on the following pages. His unit saw action at Guasimas, Kettle Hill and San Juan Hill. He mustered out with the rest of his regiment in Montauk, NY, in September of 1898. He is buried in the Fort Rosecrans National Cemetery in San Diego, Calif. ▶

"Rough Rider"
Colt Artillery
Single Action

▶ The revolver, .45 caliber, 5-1/2" barrel, has a case-hardened hammer and frame. Fire-blued trigger. Left side of frame with standard U.S. markings. Cylinder with Colt factory-added 11 ahead of 6152. Hammer recess in frame with G inspector stamp. One-piece walnut grips, the left side with faint cartouche of Capt. Frank Heath under 1885 date. Sold together with original M1881 pattern black leather flap holster shortened to accommodate this early artillery revolver. Body of holster embossed with US. Under the flap in period black ink is the name, "Rockland Colton Reed" and the stamped letters reading, "HSVC." **$32,000**

Engraved Colt Single Action Army Revolver

This SAA, SN 155296, .45 Colt, comes with silver finish, 5-1/2" barrel, full front sight and one-line block letter address with cal marking on left side. Left side of frame has two-line three-patent dates and Rampant Colt in circle. Mounted with two-piece pearl grips with deep relief carved Mexican eagle on right side. Revolver is engraved by Cuno Helfricht in his usual foliate arabesque patterns with punch dot backgrounds. The backstrap is engraved in period block letters "F.H. LANCASTER" with the date "18" near the top of the backstrap and "90" at the heel. A Colt Factory Letter states revolver was sold to Charles Hummel and Son, San Antonio, Texas, and shipped March 19, 1894. The Mexican eagle motif grips were extremely popular in Texas, and likely were supplied by the Hummel Company. It is also likely that the inscription was applied by a local San Antonio jeweler. Fred H. Lancaster was a famous Texas lawman of the late 19th and early 20th Centuries and may be the only lawman who, at various times throughout his career, held the positions of Deputy Sheriff, Deputy Federal Marshall, Chief of Police of San Antonio, and Texas Ranger. **$40,250**

Colt Single Action Revolver of Lawman Jeff Milton

This extremely rare factory engraved Colt Single Action Army Sheriff's Model Revolver, SN 333342, .45 Colt, was owned by famed lawman Jeff Milton. The revolver has a 4-3/4" barrel, made without ejector housing. It is factory engraved by Cuno Helfricht with about 80% coverage on frame consisting of intertwined foliate arabesque patterns with punch dot background. Accompanied by a Colt factory letter identifying this revolver, as found, in caliber 45 Colt with 4-3/4" barrel, blue finish, pearl stocks with carved eagle motif, factory engraved and under special features: "furnished without an ejector", sold to J.D. Milton and shipped to A. Steinfeld and Co., Tucson, Ariz., on Aug. 7, 1916 in a one-gun shipment. Milton apparently carried this gun, a cut-down .45, in a shoulder holster under his shirt. Milton served as a Texas Ranger, cowboy detective, agent for Wells Fargo, and deputy U.S. Marshall. He earned a reputation for speed and accuracy with a six-shooter. ▶

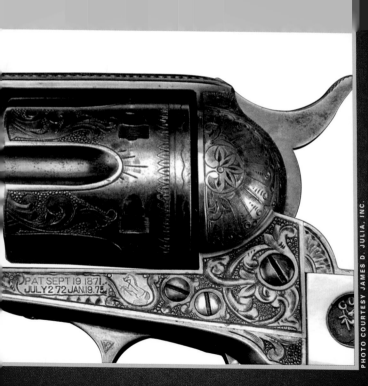

PAT SEPT 19 1871.
JULY2 72 JAN.19.75.

▶ In 1904 he was commissioned directly by President Theodore Roosevelt into the newly formed Immigration Service (USIS), where for the next 28 years he patrolled the southwestern border apprehending smugglers and illegal aliens and is recognized as being the first Immigration Border Patrolman. In March 1915, Congress authorized a separate group of inspectors called mounted guards or mounted inspectors who operated from El Paso, Texas. These guards, who never numbered more than 75, rode on horseback and patrolled as far west as California with Milton leading the way. Milton was a true western lawman who was involved in more gunfights than many famous gunfighters of his day. He was quoted as saying "I never killed a man that didn't need killing." **$201,250**

Pre-WWII Colt Single Action Army Revolver, Texas History

This revolver, SN 337150, .45 Colt, is blue and color case hardened with 4-3/4" barrel, full thick front sight and two-line address with caliber marking on left side. Left side of frame has two-line three-patent dates with rampant Colt. ▶

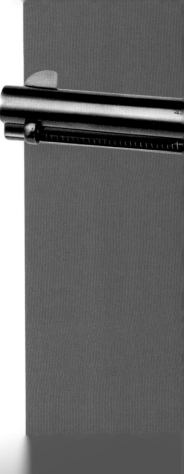

$10,350

▶ SN was observed in the usual three places on bottom of revolver. Mounted with rampant Colt hard rubber grips with the last four digits of the matching SN scratched inside each grip. Accompanied by an original factory, dark maroon, hinged lid box with correct dark blue and white end label which indicates rubber grips and blue finish. Bottom of box is inscribed with the SN "351722".

Inside the lid has an original Colt label inscribed in ink "GEO. S. WILSON / N.T.A.C." along with what appears to be an Arabic script notation. Colt Factory letter identifies revolver shipped to Momsen, Dunnigan, Ryan Co, El Paso, Texas, on April 15, 1918, in a 10-gun shipment. Mechanics are crisp, brilliant shiny bore. Box shows heavy wear with repaired corners. **$10,350**

Engraved Nickel Colt Single Action Army Revolver

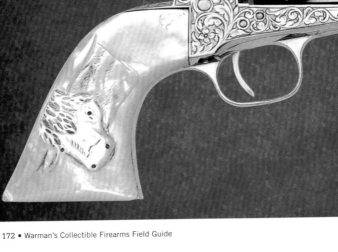

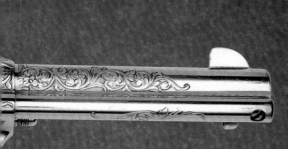

This Wilbur Glahn engraved SAA, SN 347911, .38-40, comes with a 4-3/4" barrel with top marked "COLT'S PT F.A. MFG. CO./HARTFORD CT. U.S.A." The left side of frame has three patent dates in two lines to the left of rampant Colt motif. Wilbur Glahn engraving on barrel, cylinder, ejector rod housing, back strap and trigger strap. The gun is fitted with two-piece mother of pearl carved steerhead grips. Accompanied by Colt Manufacturing Factory letter confirming gun as described and indicating it was shipped to Albert Steinfeld and Company, Tucson, Ariz., Oct. 14, 1925. **$39,675**

Engraved Colt Single Action Army Revolver

This first generation Colt revolver, SN 349941, .32 WCF (32-20) is blue and color case hardened with 7-1/2" barrel, slightly altered front sight, one-line block letter address and cal marking on left side. Left side of frame has two-line three-patent dates with Rampant Colt. Mounted with two-piece silver medallion ivory grips with raised carved ox head on right side. Revolver engraved by Wilbur Glahn in about C coverage of his distinctive intertwined foliate and floral arabesque patterns with fine punch dot background. Colt Factory letter notes gun shipped to R.S. Elliott Arms Co., Kansas City, Miss., Oct. 12, 1926. CONDITION: Extremely Fine. **$51,750**

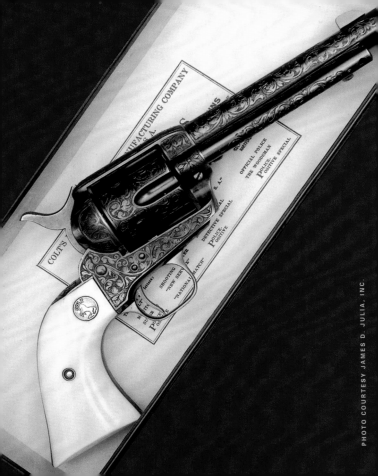

Pre-War Colt Single Action Army Revolver

This fine, engraved and inscribed revolver, SN 354968, .38 caliber, is blue and color case hardened with 5-1/2" barrel, full thick front sight with one-line block letter address and model and caliber marking on left side. Left side of frame has two-line three-patent dates and rampant Colt. Mounted with smooth two-piece silver Colt medallion ivory grips. Revolver is engraved by Wilbur Glahn with C+ or D quality engraving of foliate and floral patterns with fine stippled background. Backstrap panel engraved "H.F. Hirte". Accompanied by original dark maroon, hinged lid box. Colt Factory letter identifies revolver sold and shipped to Hans F. Hirte, San Diego, Calif., on Oct., 27, 1933. **$54,625**

Pre-War Factory Engraved Colt Single Action Army Revolver

The Colt Single Action Army (SAA), or Peacemaker as it is sometimes referred to, is one of the most widely collected and recognized firearms in the world. This rare pre-war SAA, SN 357177, is a .357 Magnum. It comes blue and color case hardened with 4-3/4" barrel, slightly altered front sight and two-line address with model and caliber marking on left side. Left side of frame has two-line three-patent dates and rampant Colt. Mounted with spectacular 2-piece pearl grips with raised carved steerhead on right side that has red stone eyes. Revolver is factory engraved by master engraver Wilbur Glahn. A Colt factory letter states the production book shows it was factory engraved on Feb. 27, 1940 and sent to the shipping room on March 30, 1940.
$43,125

Colt Model 1877 "Lightning" D.A. Revolver

The Lightning was Colt's first production of a double action revolver. Made from 1877 to 1909 with a total production of 166,849. Sales of the gun were impressive but the mechanism was rather intricate and samples are often found malfunctioning. The similarity of barrel and frame to the Single Action Army is part of the Lightning Model's appeal to collectors, as is the distinct bird's head grip profile. "Billy the Kind" (William Bonney) carried the Lightning the night he was shot by Pat Garrett. This engraved revolver, SN 19807, .38 Colt, nickel finish with 2-1/2" barrel, has full front sight and two-line address with etched panel on left side. Mounted with impressive checkered two-piece pearl grips. Revolver has full coverage New York style engraving, probably from the L.D. Nimschke shop, consisting of foliate arabesque patterns with fine stippled background. **$39,100**

Colt Sheriff's Model D.A. Revolver

A Colt Factory Letter identifies this revolver as being shipped to George E. Pond, address unknown, on June 14, 1877. This Sheriff's Model, SN 1389, .38 Colt, has nickel finish with 3-1/2" barrel, full front sight and two-line address with crisp etched panel on left side "COLT D.A. 38". Left side of frame has three-line patent dates. Mounted with one-piece checkered walnut grip matching numbered to this revolver. Trigger and edges of hammer and the screws are all bright fire blued. Sides of hammer are polished bright. Overall retains virtually all of its strong original nickel with some handling dulling; etched panel on barrel is crisp and clear; screws, trigger and hammer retain about all of their bright original fire blue. **$11,500**

Colt Model 1877 "Thunderer" Double Action Revolver

Extremely rare, factory engraved Model 1877, SN 6751, .41 Colt, nickel finish with 6" barrel, full front sight, two-line Hartford address and crisp "COLT D.A. 41" etched panel on left side.

PHOTO COURTESY JAMES D. JULIA, INC.

The Model 1877 was Colt's first attempt at manufacturing a double action revolver. Sales were brisk with more than 166,000 produced between 1877 and 1909. Model 1877 revolvers are rarely found with high original finish as they were very popular and usually saw hard service on the American frontier with infrequent or no maintenance. Many individuals on both sides of the law carried Model 1877, including Billy the Kid. This gun is mounted with original factory smooth pearl grips. Colt factory letter identified this revolver shipped on June 10, 1878. **$43,125**

Colt Model 1878 "Frontier" D.A. Revolver

The Model 1878 "Frontier" Double Action Revolver was made from 1878 to 1905 with a total production run of 51,210. This Frontier, SN 40508, is a .32 WCF (32-20), blue finish with 7-1/2" barrel, full front sight and one-line block letter address with caliber marking on left side. Left lower rear side of frame has rampant Colt in a circle and there is a swivel in the butt. Mounted with two-piece smooth ivory grips. Colt Factory letter states revolver was shipped to Schoverling, Daily and Gales, New York, NY, on April 24, 1899 in a one-gun shipment. **$6,900**

Rare Colt Flattop
Target Revolver

A highly prized variation of the Single Action Army Revolver, only 925 Flattops were manufactured from 1888 to about 1896. This revolver, SN 317922, .44 Russian, is one of only 51 of its caliber made. It features all blue finish with 7-1/2" barrel, square base target front sight, one-line block letter address and cal marking on left side. Frame has a flattop strap with target rear sight and has two-line three-patent dates on left side with Rampant Colt in broken circle. Mounted with two-piece Rampant Colt hard rubber grips that have turned chocolate. **$21,850**

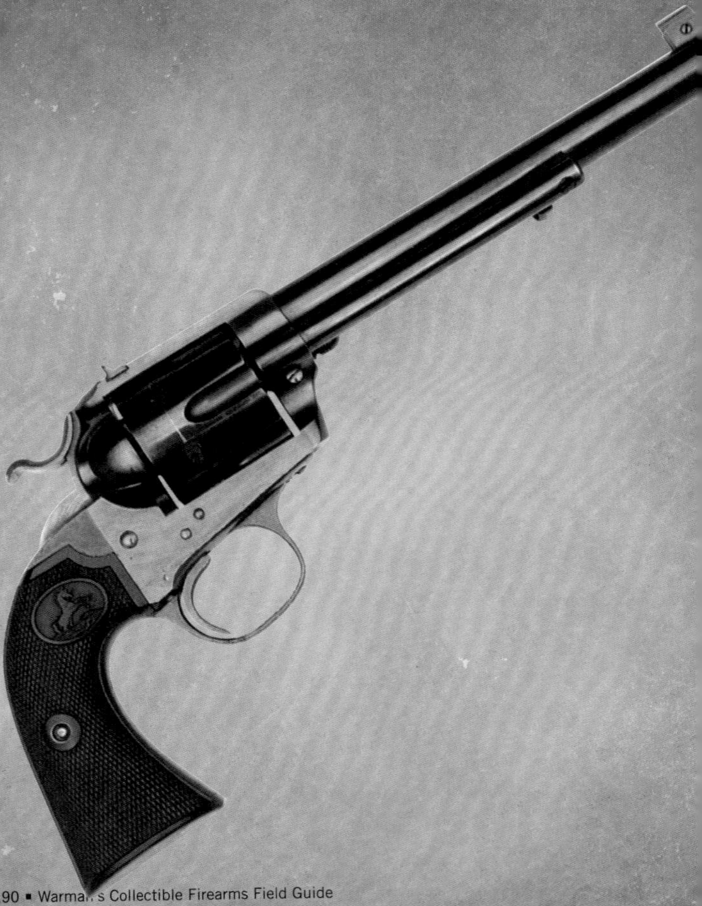

Colt Bisley Flattop Target Revolver

From 1894 to 1913, Colt produced about 976 of the Bisley Flattop Target SAA. This revolver, SN 313441, .38 WCF (38-40) is even more rare, with a total of 98 made in this caliber. All blue finish with 7-1/2" barrel, German silver target front sight and one-line block letter address, left side marked "(BISLEY MODEL) 38 W.C.F." Left side of frame has two-line three-patent dates and Rampant Colt in circle. Top strap is flat with target rear sight. Mounted with two-piece Rampant Colt hard rubber grips that have the last four digits of SN scratched inside each grip. Colt Factory letter states gun was shipped to Schwabacher Hardware, Seattle, Wash., on Dec. 22, 1910.
$13,800

PHOTO COURTESY JAMES D. JULIA, INC

Colt Bisley Model Flattop Target Revolver

Only 976 Colt Bisley Target Model Revolvers were produced from 1894-1913. This revolver, SN195344, was made in 1900 and is one of 64 Bisley Target Model revolvers chambered for the .44 S&W cartridge. The revolver has the distinctive Bisley Target Model features which include: flat top strap and sides fitted with dovetail mounted target rear sight, solid front sight base with ▶

► adjustable nickel-silver blade, Bisley "Humpback" grip and back strap, curved wide hammer with knurled spur, curved wide trigger with smooth face and black hard rubber checkered "Humpback" Bisley two-piece grips with the Rampant Colt trademark in an oval at the top of the grip. The revolver has the Colt high polish commercial blue finish with color casehardened hammer and niter blue rear sight, trigger and screws. The top of the barrel is roll-stamped with the legend "COLT'S PT. F.A. MFG. Co. HARTFORD CT. U.S.A." in one line. The left side of the barrel is roll-stamped "(BISLEY MODEL) FOR 44 S & W CTG." in one line.

$40,250

Engraved Colt Frontier Six Shooter

This rare, engraved single action revolver, SN 53117, .44 WCF (44-40) is a great find for collectors. Several thousand were made between 1878-1882 with the legend "COLT FRONTIER SIX SHOOTER" acid-etched on the left side of the barrel. These acid-etched revolvers are serial numbered 45000-65000. This revolver has nickel finish with 7-1/2" barrel, full front sight and one-line block letter address with etched panel on left side. Mounted with fine one-piece ivory grip.

Serial number is found in usual three places, on the frame, trigger guard and buttstrap with last 4 digits of SN on bottom of barrel under the ejector rod housing and on cylinder. Revolver is engraved in New York style, probably from the Nimschke shop. Colt Factory letter states gun was shipped to B. Kittredge and Co., Cincinnati, Ohio, on May 3, 1880, with 10 guns of same type. **$43,125**

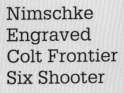

Nimschke
Engraved
Colt Frontier
Six Shooter

This SAA revolver, SN 92049, .44 WCF (44-40), features nickel finish with 5-1/2" barrel, full front sight, one-line block letter address and etched panel on left side "COLT FRONTIER SIX SHOOTER". Left side of frame has three-line patent dates and left front web of trigger guard is marked "44 CF". Mounted with two-piece pearl grips with raised carved intertwined initials which appear to be "TCE" or a combination of those three initials. Revolver is engraved by renowned master engraver L.D. Nimschke in about D coverage of foliate arabesque patterns with punch dot background on the frame which extends over both sides of barrel and each side of muzzle. This is a fine early Nimschke engraved single action. Colt Factory information identifies revolver being shipped to Hartley and Graham, New York, NY, on May 9, 1883, in a five-gun shipment. **$24,150**

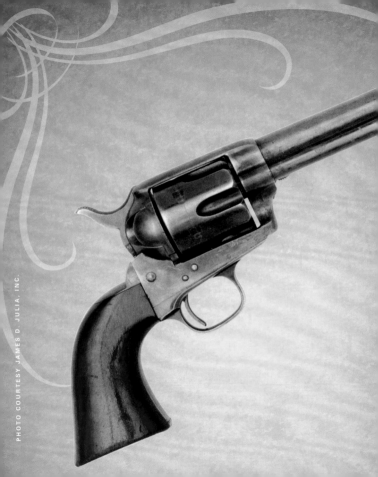

Colt Frontier Six Shooter

This Single Action Army Revolver, SN 67007, .44 WCF (44-40) is blue and color case hardened with 7-1/2" barrel, full front sight and block letter one-line address. Left side of barrel has a fully legible etched panel "COLT FRONTIER SIX SHOOTER". Bottom of barrel has last four digits of SN under ejector housing and a tiny "44" just forward of the base pin. Left side of frame has 3-line patent dates and the left front web of trigger guard is marked "44 CF". Mounted with one-piece varnished walnut grip. Etched panel single action revolvers, while not scarce, are rarely found with any original blue. Barrel retains 50-60% glossy original blue with the loss areas mostly flaked, not worn, to a light patina with light wear around the muzzle. Frame retains about 70% original case colors, strong and bright in sheltered areas, fading to silver elsewhere. **$11,500**

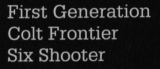

First Generation
Colt Frontier
Six Shooter

Engraved Single Action Army revolver, SN 309679, .44 WCF (44-40), bright, high luster blue and color case hardened with 7-1/2" barrel, full front sight and one-line block letter address, roll marked on left side "COLT FRONTIER SIX SHOOTER". Left side of the frame has 2-line 3-patent dates and Rampant Colt in broken circle. Mounted with 2-piece smooth ivory grips with deep left and right Colt medallions. This revolver is unusual with a nicely engraved barrel and cylinder with no engraving on frame, grip frame or ejector housing. Engraving consists of foliate arabesque patterns with punch dot background on both sides of barrel and both sides at muzzle. Barrel address is surrounded by a line border that terminates in geometric patterns with additional geometric patterns around front sight. Cylinder is engraved with foliate arabesque patterns on lands between flutes and at rear of each flute. **$28,750**

First Generation Colt Frontier Six Shooter

This Six Shooter, SN 246594, .44 WCF (44-40), is blue and color case hardened with 4-3/4" barrel, full front sight with two-line address and left side roll marked "COLT FRONTIER SIX SHOOTER". Left side of frame has two-line three-patent dates and Rampant Colt in circle. Mounted with two-piece smooth pearl grips. Barrel and ejector rod housing retain virtually all of their crisp, glossy, original factory blue with only faint sharp edge wear at muzzle and tip of ejector rod housing. Frame retains brilliant case colors. Hammer retains virtually all of its brilliant case colors. Trigger guard and backstrap retain brilliant blue in sheltered areas with the front and backstraps flaked and thinning. Mechanics are crisp, brilliant shiny bore, probably unfired. Bore and chambers of cylinder retain virtually all original factory blue. **$12,650**

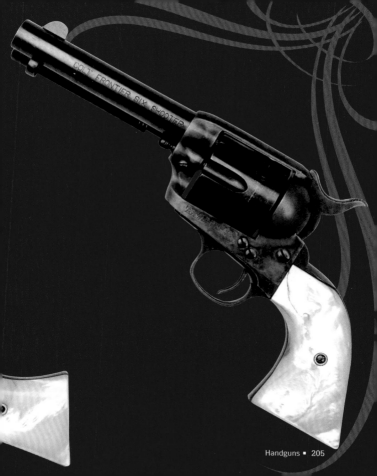

Colt Model 1902 Military Pistol

According to *Flayderman's Guide to Antique American Firearms* there were about 18,000 of these fine pistols produced from 1902-1929. They remained in service, however, well into the 1950s with target shooters because of their reliability and inherent accuracy. They were ultimately supplanted by the advent of 1911s and other newer models. This Model 1902, SN 35560, .38 caliber with blue finish, 6" barrel, fixed sights with slide stop on left side and a lanyard swivel in left heel. Mounted with two-piece smooth factory ivory grips with deep left and right Colt medallions. This is a standard production model with rear slide serrations and spur type hammer. Accompanied by one original, unmarked, all blue magazine. **$8,050**

Colt Model 1905
Semi-Auto Pistol

Only about 6,100 of these rare pistols were produced from 1905-1911, according to *Flayderman's Guide to Antique American Firearms*. This Model 1905, SN 3209, .45 caliber, with blue finish and 5" barrel, has fixed sights. Slide has standard markings on both sides with rampant Colt in a circle at left rear end. Mounted with diamond checkered walnut grips and accompanied by one original, unmarked, all-blue magazine. Backstrap is slotted for a shoulder stock. **$14,375**

Colt Model 1908 Hammerless .25

This was the smallest automatic Colt made. It is chambered for the .25 ACP cartridge, has a 2" barrel and is 4.5" long overall, weighing only 13 ounces. This is a true pocket pistol. The detachable magazine holds six shots. Approximately 409,000 were manufactured between 1908 and 1941. This factory engraved model, SN 373893, comes with a presentation box. Pistol is lightly engraved in foliate arabesque patterns with running leaf and vine borders down each side of slide. The pistol appears to be new and unfired retaining virtually all of its original Colt factory finish with bright blue and brilliant case colors. The pistol is mounted with two-piece smooth pearl grips with silver rampant Colt medallions. Pistol is accompanied by original black leatherette covered, blue velvet lined hard presentation box. Interior of lid is lined in blue satin with the stylized "COLT" logo embossed in gold. Gun was shipped June 5, 1928. CONDITION: Extremely Fine. **$8,050**

Colt New Service Model 1909 D.A. Martial Revolver

This is an exceptional U.S.M.C. Colt New Service Model 1909 Double Action Martial Revolver, SN 24639, .45 Colt, with a 5-½" barrel standard address. Blued finish. Checkered walnut grips. Martially marked on butt, dated lanyard ring. Manufactured in 1910. A total of 1,300 of this model were manufactured for the United States Marine Corps. Condition: Excellent to mint with minor flaking in spots on barrel and lower portion of gripstrap. Grips excellent. Action crisp. **$7,475**

HERITAGE AUCTIONS CO.

Colt Civilian Government Model Semi-Auto Pistol

First-year production pistol, SN C1191, .45-caliber, blue finish with 5" all blue replacement barrel. Slide has the early markings with last patent date "1911" and rampant Colt in a circle on left rear end with standard markings on right side. SN is located on left forward side of frame and right forward side of frame is marked "GOVERNMENT MODEL". Mounted with smooth two-piece pearl grips and accompanied by one two-tone lanyard loop magazine. Overall retains about 95% strong original blue with slight thinning on front strap. **$5,520**

King Altered Colt Single Action Army Revolver

This factory-engraved Colt, SN 355127, is blue and color case hardened with 4-3/4" barrel, two-line address and model and caliber markings on left side. Left side of frame has two-line three-patent dates and Rampant Colt. Front sight has been replaced with a red ivory bead mirrored King front sight and top strap has been machined to accept a white outline adjustable King rear sight. Hammer spur has been altered to the King "Cockeyed" configuration with the spur widened to left side for right hand use. Revolver has full coverage Wilbur Glahn foliate arabesque engraving with fine punch dot background. Ejector housing, cylinder, front and backstraps are engraved to match. Mounted with Colt medallion two-piece ivory grips with raised carved ox head on right side. **$29,325**

PHOTO COURTESY JAMES D. JULIA, INC.

Colt Officer's Model D.A. Revolvers

A rare cased pair of factory engraved, pearl-handled, Double-Action Revolvers, SN 625164 and 16437. Neither gun appears to have been fired beyond company testing. Overall retains 99% plus crisp original factory blue on all surfaces. Grips are equally crisp and new with great fire. **$36,800**

Pre-War
Civilian
Colt Ace

PHOTO COURTESY JAMES D. JULIA, INC.

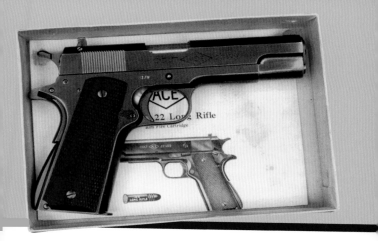

The Civilian Colt Ace was first introduced in 1931. Approximately 11,000 Ace pistols were manufactured until they were discontinued in 1941. This semi-automatic pistol, SN 3179, is chambered for .22 LR cartridge only. Blue finish with 4-3/4" solid barrel, thick front sight and adjustable rear sight. Slide has usual markings and it is mounted with full checkered walnut grips. Accompanied by one original two-tone civilian magazine with marked base plate. Also accompanied by an original dark maroon hinged lid cardboard box with blue and white end label and a Colt Ace owner's pamphlet along with a Colt "SPECIAL INSTRUCTIONS" pamphlet. Box has the number "2536" in pencil on bottom. Slide retains 96-97% glossy original charcoal blue.
$5,462

Pre-War Colt Super .38

This first-year, pre-war pistol, SN 948, is chambered for the .38 Super cartridge and has a magazine that holds nine rounds. Blue finish with 5" barrel, fixed sights and standard markings on both sides of slide. Mounted with spectacular pearl grips with left side having a raised carved ox head with red ruby or garnet eyes. Accompanied by one original two-tone magazine marked on base "38 AUTO COLT". Also accompanied by a pair of full checkered walnut grips branded on inside "RSR". Additionally accompanied by its original dark maroon hinged lid box with black and white end label and a matching SN in pencil on the bottom. Interior has a black and white Colt label inside the lid and the pencil notation "25.00". Bottom of box also contains an oil stained instruction pamphlet and a bi-fold color pamphlet titled "THE NEW SUPER-38" and an L-shaped screwdriver/punch combination tool. **$11,500**

This rare, possibly one-of-a-kind revolver, SN 354658, .38 caliber Special, all blue finish with 6" unmarked, tapered round barrel that has an unusual front sight with stippled rear face and fixed rear sight groove in top strap. This revolver is in the configuration of an Army Special with checkered trigger and hammer with polished sides. Mounted with deep silver medallion diamond checkered walnut grips. Medallions are left and right hand. Accompanied by its original dark maroon, hinged lid cardboard box serial numbered to this revolver. The end label is printed simply "PONY / COLT'S PATENT FIRE ARMS MFG. CO., HARTFORD, CONN., U.S.A." The left end of this label has the hand written notation in ink, "Jan. / 22 / 1945. This revolver, identified by SN, is pictured as Plate C on p. 347 of The Book of Colt Firearms. The caption states this is "a special model of the double action revolver made to renew the registration of the 'Pony' name for Colt's exclusive use. The Pony model was patented Jan. 22, 1945. To date no commercially available Colt arms have used the Pony designation." **$5,460**

Colt "Pony"
Double Action
Revolver

BONNIE PARKER · ALIAS · MRS. CLYDE BARROW.

Bonnie Parker's Colt
Detective Special

Notorious Depression-era criminal Bonnie Parker, who along with boyfriend Clyde Barrow gained fame as outlaws Bonnie and Clyde, carried this Colt Detective .38 caliber revolver at the time of her death in 1934. Parker had the gun taped to the inside of her thigh when she and Barrow were ambushed and killed by law officers on a rural road in Bienville Parish, Louisiana. Many of the guns carried by Bonnie and Clyde ended up in the estate of Texas Ranger Capt. Frank Hamer, who led the six-man posse that performed the ambush on May 23, 1934. As an unexpected bonus for his service, Hamer was promised he could take anything the outlaws had in their possession at the time of their capture. This .38 Special, concealed beneath Bonnie's red dress that morning—the same way she concealed the gun that enabled Clyde to bust out of prison in 1930—was one he kept. **$264,000**

Clyde Barrow

Clyde Barrow's
Colt Model 1911

This Model 1911 was removed from Clyde Barrow's waistband after bank robber was shot dead by Texas and Louisiana lawmen on May 23, 1934. This is a standard US Army pistol of World War I vintage, SN164070, .45 ACP. The gun once belonged to Frank Hamer, the Texas Ranger who led the ambush of Bonnie and Clyde. "Seldom did anyone ever live when Clyde got the first shot," warned a newsreel of the day. But on the day he was killed, Clyde Barrow didn't have the chance to reach for his gun, let alone shoot it. If he did, this would have been the gun that he grabbed from his waistband. Of all the guns found in their death car, this is the most closely related to Clyde Barrow and accordingly, the most fascinating and valuable. **$240,000**

DIVISION OF INVESTIGATION
U. S. DEPARTMENT OF JUSTICE
WASHINGTON, D. C.

NATIONAL MOTOR VEHICLE THEFT ACT

WANTED

MRS. ROY THORNTON, aliases BONNIE BARROW, MRS. CLYDE BARROW, BONNIE PARKER.

DESCRIPTION

Age, 23 years (1933); Height, 5 feet, 5 inches; Weight, 100 pounds; Build, slender; Hair, auburn, bobbed; origi- nally blonde; Eyes, blue; Complexion, fair; Scars and marks, bullet wound left foot next to little toe; bullet in left knee; burn scar on right leg from hip to knee; Peculiarities, walks with both knees slightly buckled.

RELATIVES:

Roy Thornton, husband, Texas State Penitentiary
Mrs. J. T. (Emma) Parker, mother, 1216 South Lamar St., Dallas, Texas
Mrs. Billie Parker Mace, sister, 1216 South Lamar St., Dallas, Texas
Hubert (Buster) Parker, brother, Gladewater, Texas
Nellie Gonzales, half-sister, Harwood, Gonzales County, Texas.

CRIMINAL RECORD

Arrested sheriff's office, Kaufman, Texas, June 16, 1932; charge, burglary; released.

WANT

CLYDE CHAMPION BARROW, aliases CLYD BAILEY, JACK HALE, ELDIN WILLIAMS, E

DESCRIPTION

Age, 23 years; Height, 5 feet bare feet; Weight, 150 pounds medium; Hair, dark brown, wa dyed black; Eyes, hazel; Com light, Scars and marks, shl with "U.S.N." on right fore girl's bust, left inner fore wound through both legs ju

RELATIVES:

Henry Barrow, father, Rural Dallas, Texas
Mrs. Cunie Barrow, mother, Dallas, Texas
L. C. Barrow, brother, Co Dallas, Texas
Marie Barrow, sister, Rur Dallas, Texas
Mrs. Artie Winkler, sist Apartments, Dallas, T
Mrs. Nellie Cowan, siste Apartments, Dallas,
Mrs. Jim Muckelroy, aun Mrs. Bella Briggs, aunt Frank Barrow, uncle, Ea Texas
Jim Barrow, uncle, Str D. Brown, cousin, Mart Bertha Graham, cousin, Claud Linthicum, cous Ronnie Linthicum, cou

CRIMINA

Criminal record and f tained from Ident issued October 24

Clyde Champion Barrow and Bonnie Parker constantly travel together and extreme caution must be exerci as they are wanted in connection with assault and murder of officers.

Complaint was filed at Dallas, Texas, on May 20, 1933, charging Clyde Champion Barrow and Bonnie Park Coupe, Motor No. A-1878100, property of Dr. E. L. Damron of Effingham, Illinois, from Dallas, Texas, to Pe about September 16, 1932.

Law enforcement agencies kindly transmit any additional information or criminal record to the neares investigation, U. S. Department of Justice.

If apprehended, please notify the Director, Division of Investigation listed on the back hereof which i Special Agent in Charge of the office of the Division of Investigation.

(over)

Issued by: J. EDGA

Death Car

Bonnie and Clyde Wanted Poster and Death Car

Al Capone-owned Colt Pistol

This Colt Model 1908 Vest Pocket pistol, SN 148999, .25 ACP, was owned by organized crime boss Al Capone, who through his charisma, political savvy, and sheer ruthless ambition, emerged as the most powerful and influential criminal figure of the Prohibition Era. The gun once belonged to Luigi Mascarello, a bootlegger who worked for Capone. Capone gave the pistol to Mascarello for protection. Mascarello died when his car ran into a freight train while being chased by the police. **$14,400**

Colt Python D.A. Revolver

The Python is the Cadillac of the Colt double action line. It has been manufactured since 1955. This cased and factory engraved Python, SN V 29071, .357 caliber, has a 6" barrel with ventilated rib and target sights. Profusely scroll-engraved in class D-style. Checkered factory figured-walnut grips. Left side of grip frame is marked: "COLT ENG." Contained in Colt Custom Workshop display case. Appears unfired. **$4,887**

Colt New Service Double Action Revolver Ensemble

Belonging to Tacoma, Wash., Chief of Police Anthony Zatkovich, this ensemble includes: Colt New Service Double Action Revolver, SN 332393, .45 caliber, 5-1/2" barrel. Blued finish. Faux ivory plastic grips marked, CHICAGO SPORTS, INC. 2) Tooled black leather quick release holster from Clark of Los Angeles. 3) Gold colored die cut Chief's badge. Eagle over shield pattern marked, CHIEF/POLICE/[Tacoma city seal]/TACOMA. 4) 5 x 7-inch black and white photo portrait of Zatkovich in Tacoma Police Dept uniform. 5) Zatkovich's shooter's I.D. from 1960 National Matches Camp Perry. 6) Zatkovich's Civil Air Patrol Identification Card. 7) Three newspaper articles interviewing Detective Zatkovich about his 26-year career in law enforcement. **$1,150**

Remington Beals Army
Percussion Revolver

Few Beals Army revolvers remain today with only about 1,900 produced from 1861-1862. They were virtually all issued to Union troops and saw continuous service throughout the Civil War and later on the American frontier, usually under harsh and adverse conditions with very limited or no maintenance. This revolver, SN 1173, .44 caliber has 8" octagon barrel, dovetailed German silver cone front sight with grooved top strap rear sight. Frame, barrel and cylinder are blue finished with color case hardened hammer and silver plated brass trigger guard. Mounted with smooth two-piece walnut grips numbered to revolver.
$20,700

Remington-Rider Single Shot

Also known as the "Parlor Pistol," the Single Shot was made from 1860-1863 with an estimated 200 manufactured. Very little is known about the gun.

This percussion, .17 caliber Derringer is the smallest of all Remington pistols and is not serial numbered. It has silver finish with 3" round barrel integral with frame. It has brass pin front sight and integral grips. Left side of frame is marked "RIDERS PT. / 1859". Barrel has two fine engraved zigzag lines around muzzle and a raised engraved transition from the frame to barrel. This little pistol is fitted with a reproduction removable two-piece breech which is usually missing. **$12,075**

Remington-Rider
D.A. Belt Revolver

According to *Flayderman's Guide to Antique American Firearms* only 3,000-5,000 of these revolvers were produced from 1863-1873, and of those very few were engraved. This revolver, SN 105, .36 caliber, has a 6-1/2" octagon barrel, German silver front sight and three-line address with single patent date of "SEPT. 14, 1858" and "NEW MODEL" on third line. Mounted with two-piece smooth ivory grips numbered to this revolver. Given the low SN, it is almost certain this revolver was carried by a soldier in the Civil War. Revolver is beautifully engraved, probably from the L.D. Nimschke shop, with a trophy of flags and arms with an American shield on left side and two birds on right side with foliate arabesque patterns on both sides of frame below cylinder opening. Cylinder is etch-engraved with Confederate and Union horsemen shooting at each other with trees and shrubbery. **$8,625**

Engraved Remington-Rider Pocket Revolver

An estimated 2,000 32RF metallic cartridge Remington-Rider Pocket Revolvers were manufactured after 1873. Joseph Rider of Newark, Ohio, designed this distinctive double action revolver for Remington. This rare factory engraved Pocket Revolver features ivory grips. This factory metallic cartridge conversion revolver features a factory scroll and punch dot engraving on the frame and cylinder with engraved accents on the top strap, around the hammer and back strap. The barrel has wedges of scrollwork and geometric patterns that alternate on the flats at the breech and muzzle. The silver trigger guard has an engraved star burst. **$2,185**

PHOTO COURTESY JAMES D. JULIA, INC.

Remington Vest Pocket Pistol No. 3

Also known as the "Saw Handle Deringer", less than 15,000 of these pistols were manufactured from 1865-1888. This pistol, SN 4673, .41 rimfire, has a 4" part octagon/part round barrel; termed their "No. 3" size by the factory. Left top flat is engraved "JAS. KERR and CO." and the right top flat is engraved with that company's address. Left flat of the barrel has British proofs. It has usual configuration and is mounted with two-piece rosewood grips. Few survive today. Appears to be new and unfired with only minor flaking on each side of the frame and a few small spots on bottom of barrel; grips are sound with only one minor nick and retain about all of their original bright varnish. Mechanics are crisp; brilliant shiny bore. **$19,550**

Remington Model 1875 Single Action Army

According to *Flayderman's Guide to Antique American Firearms*, only about 25,000-30,000 Model 1875s were produced from 1875 to 1889. These Remington revolvers were popular with their users but they arrived late on the market. Given Colt's head start with their Model 1873 and government contracts, along with Colt's advanced distribution system, the Remingtons were never plentiful on the frontier. Neither was Remington successful in obtaining government contracts, although 1,000 were purchased by the Mexican government. Not many Model 1875s were engraved and few are known today, especially with high original finish. Given their usual hard service on the American frontier under adverse conditions usually with little or no maintenance very few survive today with any original finish at all. This engraved Model 1875, SN 1296, .44 WCF (44-40) is nickel finished with 7-1/2" barrel, slightly altered front sight and one-line left hand Remington address. Mounted with smooth two-piece ivory grips. **$17,250**

Remington Model 1875 Single Action Army

Also known as the Improved Army or Frontier Army, the Model 1875 Revolver was manufactured from 1875 to 1889 with between 25,000 to 30,000 produced. This example offers scarce factory blue finish as most were nickel-plated. The hammer is case hardened with knurled spur. The top of the barrel is marked "E. REMINGTON & SON, ILION, N.Y. U.S.A." and the left side of the frame on the front flat is marked "44" for the caliber. The revolver is fitted with nicely figured two-piece varnished grips, which are numbered to the gun. The Model 1875 was Remington's attempt to compete with the Colt Single Action Army revolver. **$14,950**

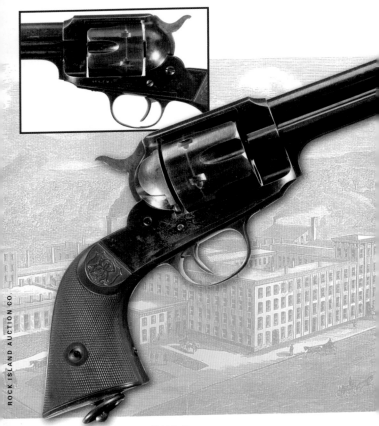

Remington Model 1890 Single Action Army

This is one of the estimated 2,000 Model 1890 Single Action Army Revolvers manufactured from 1891 to 1896. The Model 1890 was the successor to the Model 1875 and was intended to be the competitor of the Colt Single Action Army. This scare model revolver is one of the most sought after of all of the Remington produced handguns by collectors. The top of the barrel is marked "REMINGTON ARMS CO. ILION, N.Y." and "44 C.F.W." on the left side of the frame just below the cylinder. The serial number is stamped on the left side of the frame under the grip. The revolver has blade front and frame notch rear sights, lanyard stud with ring mounted on the butt and fitted with checkered grips with the "RA" monogram at the top. Compounding its rarity is its exceptional blue finish. Remington was known to have an extremely fragile bluing process which caused the blue to flake off prematurely. **$25,875**

Remington New Model Army Revolver

This rare engraved revolver, SN 34, .44 caliber, with silver and blue finish, comes with 8" octagon barrel, pinched post front sight and three-line address. Mounted with two-piece smooth ivory grips. Revolver is beautifully engraved in New York style, probably from the Nimschke shop, with about 50% coverage well executed foliate arabesque pattern with fine punch dot background. Few of this popular Civil War revolver were ever engraved, still fewer were plated. To find one today in fine original condition is rare. Revolver retains virtually all of its original silver finish, darkly oxided in several places. Rammer handle and cylinder retain most of original factory blue. Grips are sound with a few age lines and retain a fine medium ivory patina. Mechanics are crisp; brilliant shiny bore. Chambers of cylinder retain most original blue, indicating this revolver is probably unfired. **$28,750**

Remington Rider Magazine Pistol

This Joseph Rider invention is one of the most unusual of 19th century pocket pistols and one of the first metallic cartridge weapons using a tubular magazine. About 15,000 pistols were manufactured from 1871 to 1888. They were no serial numbers. This pistol, .32 rimfire extra-short, is from the famous Karl Moldenhauer Collection. Blue and color case hardened with 3" octagon barrel, German silver half moon front sight with magazine tube integral with the bottom flat, the pistol is mounted with two-piece smooth walnut grips. Bottom of buttstrap is marked "KM76" in white paint, the inventory number from the Moldenhauer Collection. Blue and color casehardened examples of this pistol are considered rare. **$20,700**

Texas Ranger Collection

Lot of Remington Semi-Automatic Pistol, hat, badges and ephemera belonging to Texas Ranger Johnny Krumnow, including: 1) Remington Rand Model 1911 Semi-Automatic Pistol, SN 1338081, .45 caliber, 5-inch barrel; 2) Stetson hat, marked in ink inside sweatband: Sgt. Johnny Krumnow Texas Ranger Co. A; 3) 1-7/8" diameter circle and star badge marked: Texas/[state flag]/Ranger; 4) Department of Public Safety Special Texas Ranger identification card; 5) Business Card of Krumnow as Private Investigator; 6) Lieutenant badge from Harris County Sheriff's Dept. **$1,195**

Smith & Wesson
1st Model 3rd Issue

Manufactured between 1868 and 1882, the 1st Model 3rd issue was the last of the tip-up style revolver produced by Smith & Wesson. This revolver, SN 160801, .22 Short rimfire, nickel finish, has a 3-1/4" keyhole shape barrel, half moon front sight and 1-line address. It has seven-shot cylinder and is fitted with two-piece birdhead smooth ivory grips. Revolver is engraved by renowned engraver L.D. Nimschke with about 40-50% coverage foliate arabesque patterns with punch dot background on frame. Sides of barrel are engraved with foliate arabesque patterns at each end with double snake and dot patterns in between. Top of backstrap has Nimschke's distinctive crossed ribbon patterns with punch dot background and a foliate spray on back strap. Cylinder is engraved with foliate arabesque patterns on the lands between the flutes. Accompanied by an original red felt lined rosewood casing. Revolver retains virtually all of its strong original nickel finish and is probably unfired. Mechanics are crisp, brilliant shiny bore with a few spots of pitting. **$6,900**

Dubbed the "American," the .44 gauge revolver with an 8"
barrel was the first such gun to be adopted by the United States
military. It was made from 1872-1874, with about 20,735
produced. The revolver is identified by the interlocking hammer
and latch, and a bump in the bottom of the frame just above the
trigger. The top of the barrel rib is marked "+SMITH & WESSON
SPRINGFIELD MASS. U.S.A PAT. JULY10. 60. JAN 17. FEB 17.
JULY 11. 65 & AUG. 24. 69+". The serial number is marked on
the butt with the matching assembly number "405" on the rear
cylinder face and barrel latch. Blue finish with casehardened
hammer and trigger guard, blade front and notch rear sights and
fitted with smooth walnut grips. **$23,000**

Smith & Wesson "Second Model American"

Long associated with the American West, this is an exceptional example of a Smith & Wesson No. 3 Second Model American Single Action Revolver.

PHOTO COURTESY JAMES D. JULIA, INC.

Smith &
Wesson No. 3
Second Model
Single Action

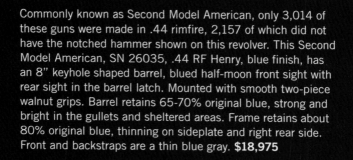

Commonly known as Second Model American, only 3,014 of these guns were made in .44 rimfire, 2,157 of which did not have the notched hammer shown on this revolver. This Second Model American, SN 26035, .44 RF Henry, blue finish, has an 8" keyhole shaped barrel, blued half-moon front sight with rear sight in the barrel latch. Mounted with smooth two-piece walnut grips. Barrel retains 65-70% original blue, strong and bright in the gullets and sheltered areas. Frame retains about 80% original blue, thinning on sideplate and right rear side. Front and backstraps are a thin blue gray. **$18,975**

Smith & Wesson Model 3 Russian Third Model

This rare, engraved S&W, SN 49727, .44 Russian, features silver and gold finish with 6-1/2" keyhole shape barrel, integral front sight and one-line address with last patent date "AUG 24 69". It has the distinctive finger rest hook on trigger guard and a lanyard loop in buttstrap. Mounted with two-piece smooth pearl grips. Barrel and frame are silver finished with gold washed cylinder, hammer and trigger guard. Trigger is fire blued. Revolver has nearly full coverage spectacular, intertwined, foliate arabesque patterns by renowned master engraver L.D. Nimschke. Bottom of muzzle is engraved "L.D.N. / N.Y." There are few, if any, authenticated, signed Nimschke engraved handguns. One scroll on left side of frame terminates in a flower blossom and right side of barrel has a floral and fan pattern. Top of back strap is engraved in Mr. Nimschke's distinctive crossed ribbon pattern and with flower blossoms. **$112,125**

Smith & Wesson
.44 D.A. Frontier

The fine Double Action revolver, SN 47936, .44 Russian, features all blue finish with 6" keyhole shape barrel, half moon front sight and fixed rear sight as part of the barrel latch. Cylinder is 1-9/16" with usual six-shots and double stop notches. It is mounted with two-piece S&W logo embossed hard rubber grips matching numbered to this revolver.

Accompanied by its original hinged-lid brown cardboard box with light blue end label with black lettering. Bottom of box is pencil numbered to this revolver. Overall retains virtually all of its glossy original factory blue with only faint muzzle edge wear and minor sharp edge wear on cyl and frame. Hammer and trigger retain virtually all of their brilliant original case colors. Grips are crisp and new. Mechanics are crisp, brilliant shiny bore. Box is sound with some brown paper losses and corner wear. $13,800

Smith & Wesson
Ladysmith
1st Model D.A.

This was Smith & Wesson's first double action .22 revolver and was designed by Daniel B. Wesson specifically for women. According to *Flayderman's Guide to Antique American Firearms*, only 4,575 of this model were produced from 1902-1906. They are rarely found today with high original finish. This Ladysmith, SN 2712, .22-caliber, blue finish, has a 3-1/2" round barrel and integral half moon front sight. Left side of frame has the S&W trademark logo and a checkered, domed cylinder release button. Revolver is mounted with two-piece smooth pearl grips with deep gold S&W medallions. **$6,320**

A rare, Double Action pre-WWII registered revolver, SN 47085, .357 Magnum. Blue finish with 6-1/2" ribbed barrel, partridge front sight and adjustable rear sight in the round top strap. Top of rib and top strap are beautifully checkered. Hammer is humpback style with very fine checkered spur, serrated edges and patent registration on back edge. The registration number "600" is on the frame inside the crane. Mounted with wonderful diamond checkered, large silver medallion, magna grips. Grips are unnumbered but are original to this revolver. Accompanied by its original blue/purple two-piece box with red interior with both English and Spanish directions inside the lid. Top of the box has a gold rectangle with the image of a similar revolver along with gold embossing. Ends are also gold embossed. **$8,050**

Smith & Wesson Model 29S D.A. Revolver

This S&W Model 29S, SN S172620, .44 magnum caliber, has a 6-½" ribbed barrel with target sights. Polished blue finish. Case-hardened hammer and trigger. Four-screw frame. Lively grained checkered factory hardwood grips with medallions. Contained in original factory blue pasteboard box with brass latch. Sold together with untouched original tools which are fixed to the blue interior with white elastic. **$2,031**

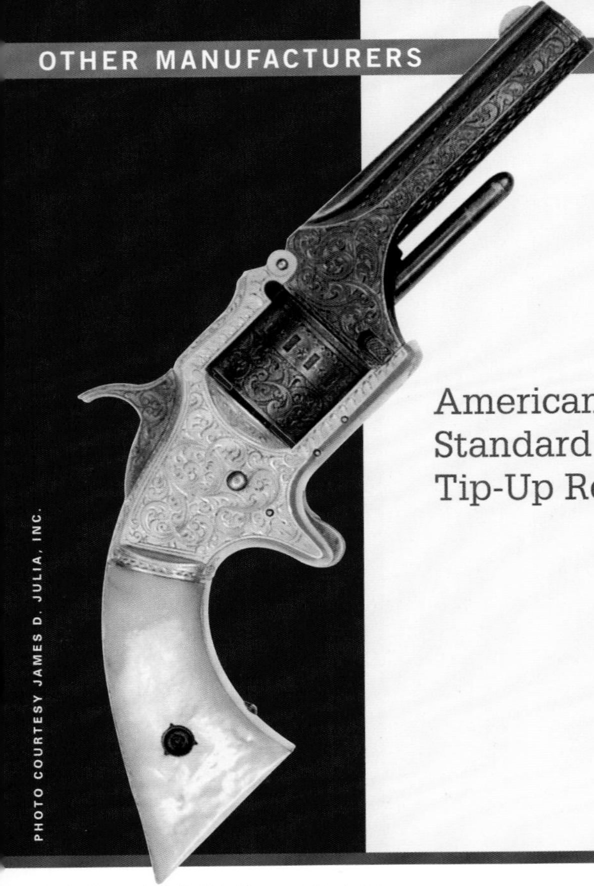

PHOTO COURTESY JAMES D. JULIA, INC.

American Standard Tool Tip-Up Revolver

This cased engraved pistol, SN 7, .22-caliber, has all the appearances and attributes of a Smith & Wesson First Model 2nd Issue type .22 revolver. It has blue and gold finish with 3-1/8" octagon, keyhole shape barrel with half moon German silver front sight and "AMERICAN STANDARD TOOL Co. NEWARK N.J." address. Mounted with two-piece smooth, pearl grips serial numbered to this revolver. Cylinder is seven-shots with double front stop notches. Revolver is engraved by master engraver L.D. Nimschke. Given the quality and profusion of the engraving along with the gold plating and fine blue finish, with pearl grips and deluxe casing along with the single-digit SN, this was undoubtedly an exhibition piece for the company. Accompanied by its original rosewood case with a cartridge block in left front for 51 cartridges. **$23,000**

Ames Boxlock Pistols 1842 Dated

This rare cased pair of pistols are believed to have been presented to George C. Reed, who served as captain and in command of the U.S.S. Constitution, 1825. Reed was eventually promoted to Rear Admiral and died in 1862. The pistols have 6" round barrels, marked at the breeches "U.S.N/JCB/P" in a sunken circle with the date "1842" on both barrel tangs. These are from the very early delivery period having the pointed lock plates which are extremely rare as only the first 300 pistols delivered in 1842 were made with the pointed locks. The pistols are cased in a fitted walnut box. **$40,250**

J. H. Dance & Brothers Confederate Revolver

This rare and historic engraved Second Model J.H. Dance and Brothers Confederate Dragoon Percussion Revolver, SN 164, was exhibited at the New York Metropolitan Museum of Art in 1942. The .44 caliber revolver has an 8" octagonal barrel with a six-shot cylinder. Sides of hammer engraved with Masonic eye and arrow motifs. Rare one-piece beveled ebony grips inlaid with a last quarter moon Masonic emblem of German silver, a known symbol used by the Knights of the Golden Circle (KGC). This emblem symbolized the tearing down of an old structure to prepare the way for a new one, in this case, the regional collective belief in slavery that could not coexist with Union abolitionist policies. KGC members possessed a discontent with the existing federal government and wished to create a new country with a pro-slavery agenda. The quality and features of this revolver suggest the owner had affiliation with the KGC during the Civil War. The Dance firm started manufacturing firearms in 1862 and modeled their revolvers after the famous Colt Dragoon. The men who worked for this company were granted exemption from military service by the state because the great need for firearms. The J.H. Dance & Brothers factory, located in East Columbia, Texas, manufactured firearms exclusively for the Confederacy. Only 325 to 500 revolvers were manufactured. **$57,500**

Deringer Model
1842 Pistol

This is one of 1,200 Model 1842 Navy Percussion Pistols manufactured by Henry Deringer of Philadelphia circa 1842-1847. The Model 1842 Navy percussion pistol was the first percussion pistol manufactured and delivered under government contract and the first U.S. government handgun with a rifled barrel. This is an example of a Standard model 1842 Deringer pistol with deeply rifled, seven-groove barrel. Experts believe that Deringer manufactured fewer than 200 Standard Model 1842 Navy pistols. The lock plate is stamped "U.S./DERINGER/ PHILADELa" below the hammer. Brass post front sight on the barrel and an integral fixed rear sight on the tang. Browned barrel, bright finished swivel ramrod, hammer and lock plate, brass barrel band, trigger guard and round buttcap with a varnished walnut stock. **$5,750**

Hopkins and Allen
XL No. 8

Manufactured in the late 1870s to the early 1880s by Hopkins and Allen, Norwich, Conn., only several hundred of these revolvers are estimated to have been produced. This example, SN 408, caliber 44-40, has a 3-3/4" barrel and is nickel-plated. The revolver is mounted on walnut grips and has a lanyard on butt. Case hardened hammer and trigger guard. Fire-blued trigger. Top right frame strap is stamped "Hopkins and Allen M'fg Co. Pat. Mch 28. 71 May 27. 79". Other side is stamped with "XL No.8" and "Cal. Winchester 1873". All metal parts are engraved with diamond and floral motifs, stylized punch decorated scroll, with setter on left hand side of frame. Retains nearly all its original nickel-plate with some slight discoloration in groove at top of action, thinning a bit on grip straps. Light drag line on cylinder. Hammer and trigger guard retain most of their original case hardening color, and trigger most of its fire-blue. Grips are excellent, with a few minor marks. Bore is excellent. Action is crisp. **$9,440**

ROCK ISLAND AUCTION CO.

Krieghoff Luger
Luftwaffe-ordered

Approximately 4,500 of these Krieghoff "S" Code Lugers were manufactured for the Luftwaffe with one- to four-digit serial numbers. This Luger has the early "S" code over the chamber indicating manufacture in 1936. It has the early toggle markings with the "H/Krieghoff Anchor/K" over "SUHL". The right side of the barrel extension is marked with the early "LWaA" 1st-stage 1 early Luftwaffe acceptance proof followed by the Luftwaffe test proof and small "eagle/2" proof. The underside of the barrel is marked with only the bore diameter and the "Eagle/2" acceptance proof. It has the typical military style serial number placement with the full serial number on the front frame and the left side of the barrel extension with the last two digits on the various smaller parts. The pistol is fitted with a set of slightly thicker checkered walnut grips. The pistol is complete with one unmarked nickel plated magazine body with cast aluminum base that is numbered with the Krieghoff Luftwaffe "Eagle/2" proof over serial number "6969". **$10,350**

ROCK ISLAND AUCTION CO.

Krieghoff 1943 Luger

An excellent example of a rare WWII 1943 military contract Krieghoff P.08 Luger, complete with two matching magazines with an undated Luftwaffe "Eagle 2" proofed black leather holster. The pistol, SN 11375, 9mm caliber, has a 4" barrel. The top of the chamber is marked "1943" with the front toggle correctly marked with the late production C-2 style Krieghoff toggle marking that has the smaller "C" style radii anchor with the left point of the anchor, slightly outside the letter "H" with the right point touching the bottom of the "K". The right side of the barrel extension has the 1st "LWa" stage II early acceptance proof next to the stage II mid-proof, next to the final acceptance proof. The underside of the barrel is marked with: "188/LWa2/ serial number "11375", that is numbered in the smaller numbered size. The left side of the breechblock has the correct Luftwaffe/Eagle/2 firing proof on both sides. It is fitted with the correct late production coarse checkered black plastic grips. **$43,600**

Leech and Rigdon
Confederate Revolver

This particular revolver, SN 1290, .36 caliber, six-shot cylinder, 7-1/2" barrel, is among the finest examples of this model known. Made circa 1863-64. Gun appears 100% original and complete and has all standard features associated with these pistols made in Greensboro, Georgia. Barrel is marked "LEECH and RIGDON CSA" on top barrel flat. There is "S.CA" stamped in bottom of right stock. Cryptic of four dots in a cross is seen on right side of trigger guard. SN are found on all parts normally numbered on this gun, including barrel housing, loading arm, latch, wedge, frame, arbor, cylinder, trigger guard and backstrap. **$57,500**

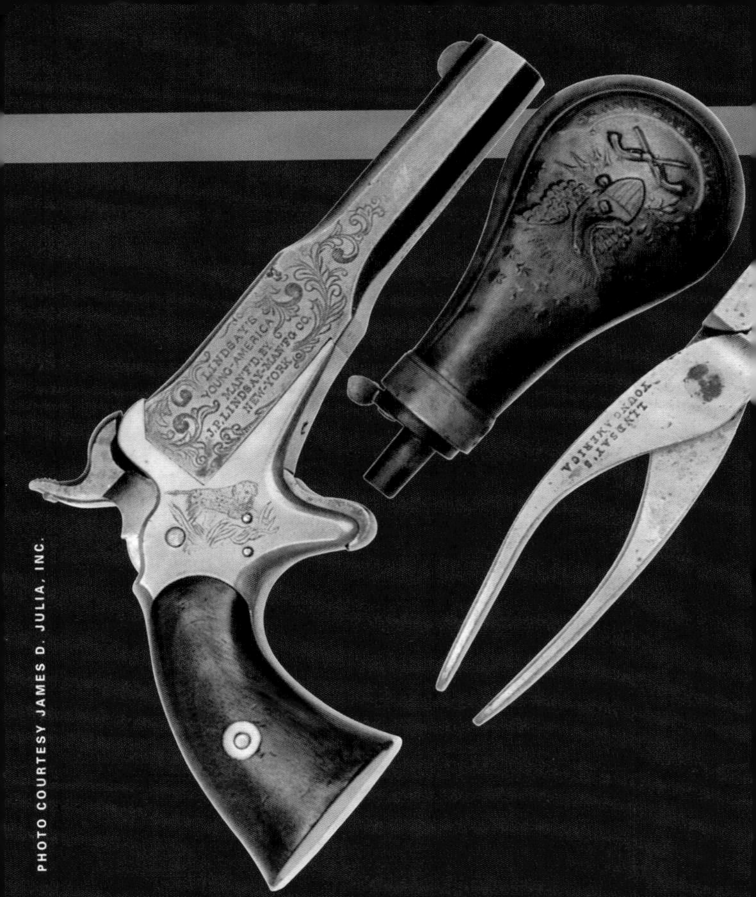

PHOTO COURTESY JAMES D. JULIA, INC.

Lindsay Two-Shot Pocket Pistol

Made by Union Knife Company, Naugatuck, Conn., for the inventor John P. Lindsay, early 1860s, this well-made pistol, SN 520, .41 caliber, has a 4" octagon barrel with scalloped top flats about half the length and half moon front sight mounted on a flat side brass frame with two hammers and spur trigger. This pistol is designed for two superposed loads with the trigger firing first one hammer and then the other. Mounted with two-piece smooth walnut grips. Left side of barrels is engraved with a trophy of flags, an eagle, a lion and a workman's arm with a hammer. Left side of frame is engraved with a bull elk. Right side of barrel has the maker's name and address. Right side of frame is engraved with a bird dog on point and it has two-line patent numbers on bottom of barrels. Accompanied by a brown leather case that has been configured and partitioned for the pistol, a small double sided eagle and shield flask marked on collar "LINDSAY'S YOUNG AMERICA" and a single cavity proprietary bullet mold marked on each handle "LINDSAY'S YOUNG AMERICA". **$4,025**

Mauser Model 96

This fixed sight, 10-shot Cone Hammer semi-automatic pistol, SN 9162, comes with a wood holster stock. The pistol, 7.63mm Mauser caliber, has a 5-1/2" barrel marked: Fabrik/ Mauser /Oberndorf. Fixed rear sight. Blued action. 10-round fixed magazine. German proof marks. 23-groove walnut grips. Wood holster stock with attaching iron marked: 9162. Condition: Excellent. **$18,975**

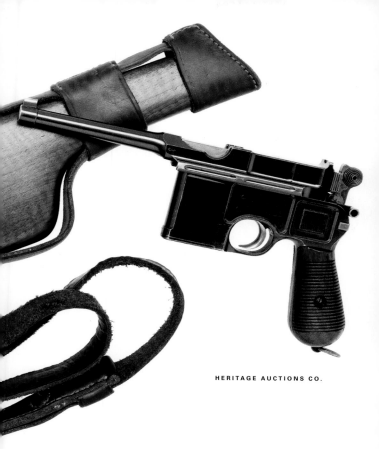

Merwin, Hulbert & Co.
1st Model Single Action
Army Revolver

PHOTO COURTESY JAMES D. JULIA, INC

According to *Flayderman's Guide to Antique American Firearms*, there were only a few thousand produced in the 1880s in five different configurations. The Merwin and Hulbert design was superior to other handguns of the period with their ease of unloading and ejecting empty casings. Closing the barrel allowed the cylinder to be reloaded through the sliding loading gate in the right recoil shield. Unfortunately Merwin and Hulbert came on the scene long after Colt and to some extent, Remington, were already in production and widely distributed. With the lack of government contracts and a weak distribution system they could not compete. A majority of Merwin and Hulbert revolvers were sold in Mexico and are rarely found today with high original finish. This revolver, SN 4462, .44 WCF (44-40), nickel finish, has a 7" round barrel, integral front sight with one-line Merwin and Hulbert address on top and Hopkins and Allen address on left side. **$9,775**

Merwin, Hulbert & Co. Spur Trigger Revolver

According to *Flayderman's Guide to Antique American Firearms* these revolvers were produced in the 1880s with an unknown quantity manufactured. Flayderman states they are "scarce" and that the scoop flute cylinders are "rare".

This revolver, SN 3628, .38 S&W, nickel finish, comes with scarce 3-3/4" keyhole shape barrel, half moon front sight and two-line Hopkins and Allen address on top of rib. It has five-shot scooped flute cylinder and is mounted with square butt hard rubber grips with deep relief dogs' heads at the top and matching numbered to this revolver. Left side of frame has the Merwin and Hulbert address and right side of frame the caliber marking. Frame has spur trigger. Revolver is spectacularly engraved, probably by master engraver Gustave Young, with extremely fine detailed foliate arabesque patterns and wavy borders around both sides. Accompanied by its original New York exhibition style hinged lid black leather covered casing with black and gold embossed lines around the lid. Bottom is recessed for the revolver and the left front is set with a cartridge block for 32 cartridges containing 31 early style beveled rim, copper primed .38 S&W cartridges. **$12,650**

James Reid
Large Frame
Knuckle-Duster

Only about 150 of these pistols were produced from 1870 to 1872, according to *Flayderman's Guide to Antique American Firearms*, making this an extremely rare American pistol. This example, SN 6040, .41 rimfire, is silver finished with silver plated brass frame and steel five-shot cylinder. Top strap is marked "J. REID'S DERRINGER" with patent date below, bottom front of frame is fitted with a sliding safety. Bottom of frame has a screw attached trap door for access to mainspring. Frame is lightly engraved in foliate arabesque patterns with a checkered oval on backstrap. Mechanics are fine, bright shiny bores, possibly

Savage Navy Percussion Civilian Revolver

This rare civilian presentation-quality deluxe revolver, SN 1296, .36 caliber, has 7-1/8" octagon barrel. Barrel, frame, cylinder and rammer housing are all deluxe high polish blue while the trigger guard, ring trigger, hammer and rammer handle are color case hardened. Mounted with deluxe, highly figured, smooth walnut two-piece grip. According to *Flayderman's Guide to Antique American Firearms*, there were about 20,000 of these revolvers produced from 1861 to mid-1860s of which about 12,000 were sold on government contract. There is no indication of the number of presentation quality revolvers produced but it is almost certainly a very limited number and of those, extremely few were cased. CONDITION: Revolver is Extremely Fine. **$46,000**

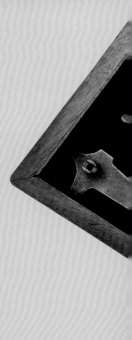

Savage Model 1907 Gold Engraved

This rare factory, gold engraved Savage pistol, SN 1, .32 caliber, features one of the more elaborate engravings, attributed to Enoch Tue. It features a full gilded finish with solid silver grips that are checkered and has Savage motif on both sides. The magazine is also gold washed. Accompanying this gun is original box with instructions. Overall condition of gun is Very Fine with 98% original gold gilding remaining. **$12,650**

"Buffalo Bill" Savage Model 1907

This factory engraved Savage Model 1907, SN 33177, .32 ACP, was presented to William Frederick "Buffalo Bill" Cody, soldier, bison hunter and showman, made world famous for his Wild West Shows, which toured Great Britain and Europe. The gun features an all blue finish with 3-3/4" barrel, fixed sights and standard markings, mounted with smooth pearl grips that have the Savage Arms Co. logo in the center. Engraved on backstrap "Col. W.F. Cody". Accompanied by a letter from noted researcher and historian, R.L. Wilson, who states the majority of known Buffalo Bill guns are in museums, unavailable to collectors. The pistol was shipped to Cody Aug. 22, 1911. **$66,125**

Sharps Model 1B 4-Barrel Deringer

According to *Flayderman's Guide to Antique American Firearms* there were about 3,200 of these little pistols produced from 1859 to 1874. Few were engraved and boxes for them are even more rare. This example, SN 2563, .22 rimfire, silver finish, has a 2-1/2" 4-barrel cluster, brass pin front sight and mounted with smooth two-piece pearl grips. Pistol has fluted standing breech with barrel release button

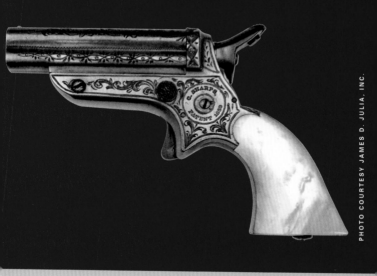

on left side and Sharps name and patent date around the hammer screw. Pistol is engraved in early foliate vine style with diamond and dot patterns on standing breech. Top of back strap is engraved in diamond and dot patterns with back strap engraved in geometric patterns. Comes with an original black two-piece cardboard box with "DIRECTIONS FOR USE OF SHARP'S PATENT REPEATER" label inside lid. **$12,650**

This is a rare example of one of the Model 1911 A1 Pistols manufactured by the Singer Manufacturing Company during WWII. There were only 500 pistols produced by Singer under the U. S. Army, Ordnance Educational Order No. W-ORD-396, with almost all of these pistols theoretically issued to the U.S. Army Air Corps. With the very low total number produced, examples are scarce in any condition. For a .45 Auto collector, this is the holy grail of all Model 1911A1 WWII pistols. The left side of the slide is marked in two lines "S. MFG. CO./ELIZABETH, N.J., U.S.A.", with no markings on the right side. The top of the slide and left side of the frame are correctly stamped with a single "P" proof mark and the slide is correctly not stamped with the pistol serial number under the firing pin retaining plate. The left side of the frame is stamped with the "JKC" initials of Col. John K. Clement, the Executive Officer of the New York Ordnance District. The right side of the frame is stamped in two lines "UNITED STATES PROPERTY/M 1911 A1 U.S.ARMY" with the serial number "No S800491" below that. The pistol has the wide spur hammer with borderless checkering, with the checkered thumb safety, slide stop, trigger and mainspring housing. **$69,000**

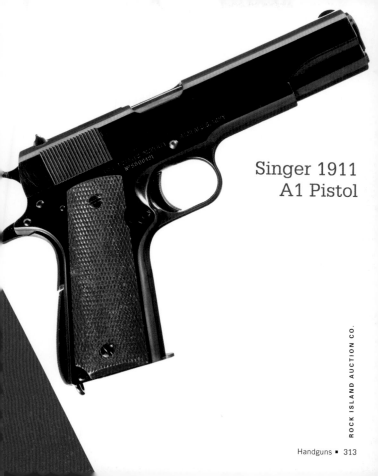

Singer 1911
A1 Pistol

Volcanic Arms No. 2
Navy Lever-Action Pistol

George E. Albee, an Indian Wars Medal Of Honor recipient, once owned this pistol, SN 1673, .41 caliber. In the fall of 1869, serving as a member of the 24th Infantry on the Western frontier fighting Indians in Texas, Lt. Albee and his unit were involved in a major conflict with hostile Indians on the Brazos River. Albee's heroic actions earned him the Medal of Honor. The pistol is the usual Navy size configuration with 8" octagon barrel, integral magazine, with German silver pin front sight and fixed rear sight. Top flat of barrel has a sharp three-line Volcanic Arms address.

Mounted with two-piece smooth varnished walnut grips. Albee apparently acquired the pistol around 1870. He died in 1918. At one point the pistol was in the collection of renowned firearms author and historian Norm Flayderman. Albee was born in New Hampshire in 1845 and enlisted in Company G Wisconsin 1st U.S. Sharpshooters (Berdan Sharpshooters) in June 1862. He retired from service in 1878. Upon retirement he was employed by Winchester in developing the Hotchkiss rifle. He became a company exhibition shooter and won the Lorillard Rapidity Match at Creedmoor, Long Island, in 1882 firing 20 shots in 60 seconds at 200 yards without a miss. **$48,875**

John Walch
Navy Model 12-Shot Revolver

The Navy Model Revolver was made from 1859 to the early 1860s in a total quantity of about 200 at the Union Knife Company, Naugatuck, Conn., according to *Flayderman's Guide to Antique Firearms*. The revolver is .36-caliber, 12-shot cylinder with six chambers, each taking a double load. This rare revolver, SN NSN, has blue finish with 6" octagon barrel, dovetail front sight and rear sight in the left hammer nose. Top of barrel is hand engraved "R. STAHL and CO = NW=YORK". It has a square butt grip frame and is mounted with smooth two-piece walnut grips. This revolver is one of America's most unusual inventions wherein the six-chambered cylinder is loaded with two superposed loads. The rear of the cylinder has two concentric rows of nipples and it has two side-by-side hammers. When the revolver is to be fired both hammers are cocked and with the first pull of the trigger the right hammer falls firing the forward load in that chamber and the second pull of the trigger fires the rear load. **$36,800**

Walther PPK,
Marshall Hermann Goering

This cased gold washed engraved .32-caliber Walther PPK, SN 408111k, together with spare clip and three rounds of ammunition were surrendered by Herman Goering at the time of his capture in early May of 1945, at the conclusion of WWII. Goering served as Commander-in-Chief of the Luftwaffe, President of the Reichstag, Prime Minister of Prussia and, as Hitler's designated successor, the second man in the Third Reich. He was cunning, brutal and ambitious. After World War II, Goering was convicted of war crimes and crimes against humanity at the Nuremberg Trials. He was sentenced to death by hanging, but committed suicide by ingesting cyanide hours before the sentence was to be carried out. **$40,250**

Wesson & Harrington No. 4, .38 Caliber

According to *Flayderman's Guide to Antique American Firearms* only about 500 of these scarce revolvers were produced in two calibers – .38 rimfire or .41 rimfire – from 1875-1877. Few were engraved or special plated; and only a handful were cased. This rare revolver, SN 112, .38 rimfire, is finished gold over nickel and has a 3-1/2" octagon barrel, German silver front sight and one-line address. It has five-shot fluted cylinder and is mounted with two-piece smooth bird head pearl grips. It is engraved in New York style, probably from the L.D. Nimschke shop with about 50% coverage fine foliate arabesque and geometric patterns. Each side of the upper front frame is engraved in diamond and dot patterns. Cylinder is engraved with foliate arabesque patterns on the lands between the flutes and has a chip and dot border at rear edge. Backstrap is engraved in period script, "Presented to Lieut. John W. Davidson / by the Officers of the 14th Police District / Philadelphia. Dec. 25th. 1875." Accompanied by its original purple velvet lined mahogany casing. **$14,950**

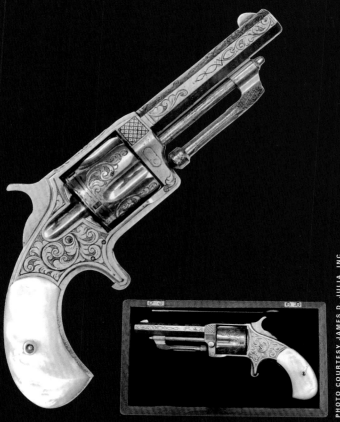

Sheriff's Badge

Gold Shield & Star Badge of B.F. Walker, Sheriff of Siskiyou Co. California. 2 ½-inches tall. The shield and pierced star badge with hard-fired black enamel ribands reading: Sheriff/B.F. Walker/ Siskiyou Co. Scroll engraved. Reverse with wide T-bar pin and tube catch. 14k. Condition: Excellent. **$5,175**

HERITAGE AUCTIONS CO.

LONG ARMS

Winchester 1860 Henry
Lever Action Rifle

Extremely fine .44 Henry rimfire standard rifle, SN 2425, with 24-1/4" octagon barrel, has integral magazine, square back, tapered, German silver front sight, an empty dovetail over the chamber area with its original 900-yard Henry ladder rear sight marked "900" at the top, in the dovetail in the top flat of the receiver. Top flat of the barrel has the usual Henry company name, patent date and address forward of the dovetail and the serial number in the usual position behind the dovetail. Mounted with straight grain, uncheckered American walnut, slight perch belly buttstock with early style round heel brass buttplate with trap that has the large cleaning rod hole containing an original 4-piece iron and hickory cleaning rod. Henry rifles of this era were very popular with Union and Confederate troops during the Civil War when they could find them. Quite a few company-size Union outfits, especially those from Kentucky, Illinois, Indiana and Missouri, purchased at their own expense, and carried, Henry rifles. They are rarely found with high original condition having served continuously throughout the Civil War and later on the American frontier, usually under adverse conditions with limited or no maintenance. **$109,250**

Engraved Winchester Henry Rifle

An extraordinary example of original deluxe factory engraved running deer panel scene Henry lever action rifle that was manufactured by the New Haven Arms Co. in late 1864 or early 1865.

Only 14,000 Henry rifles were manufactured. It is extremely rare to find one with gold plating, factory engraving, and a select grade varnished walnut stock. Most Henry Rifles were made with plain, unfinished, brass frames and buttplates. This rifle, SN 7009, was factory engraved by Samuel J. Hogson and features bordered scrollwork on a punch-dot background with grape leaf designs on the forward frame panels and a game scene with a leaping buck on the left side plate. The brass frame and buttplate are gold-plated; the barrel and integral magazine are blued and the hammer and lever are case-hardened. The rifle has a highly figured, select grade walnut stock with high polish, piano finish. The top of the barrel is roll-stamped with the two-line legend: "HENRY'S PATENT OCT. 16. 1860/MANUFACT'D BY THE NEWHAVEN. ARMS CO. NEWHAVEN. CT." ahead of the rear sight. The initials "F.G." are factory stamped on the internal left side of upper frame tang. **$184,000**

Iron Frame Winchester 1860 Lever Action Rifle

A rare iron frame Model 1860, SN 197, .44 RF Henry with 24-1/4" octagon barrel, integral magazine tube and slightly altered original German silver front sight with 1,000 yard Henry ladder rear sight, missing its slide. Receiver and sideplates are of iron with a second dovetail in the top flat of the receiver. Mounted with nicely figured, slab-sawed American walnut that has a bottom mounted sling swivel with a sling loop on right side of barrel. There were less than 400 of these iron frame Henrys produced very early in the production run with no. "355" the highest SN known. Fine to Very Fine condition. **$86,250**

Early Winchester 1860 Henry Lever Action Rifle

This very nice Henry rifle, SN 919, features the standard 24-1/4" octagon barrel, integral magazine tube, early style rounded top German silver front sight and first type 1,000-yard Henry ladder rear sight. Receiver has a second rear sight dovetail in the top flat and has the earlier sharp radius on the top rear edge. Buttstock has the early style slight perch belly and the early style brass buttplate with rounded heel and trap. Trapdoor is the larger size with a correspondingly larger hole in the buttstock for the accompanying four-piece hickory and steel wiping rod. Extremely Fine condition. Mechanics are crisp, very bright shiny bore. Barrel and magazine tube retain about 95% strong original blue. Four-piece hickory and steel wiping rod is extremely fine with a couple of minor chips. **$80,500**

Martially Marked Winchester Model 1860

This Model 1860, SN 9169, is a late or Type II martial Henry purchased by the government in about 1864 and 1865 and was part of the more than 600 Henry rifles purchased during that time frame. This rifle is listed by serial number on p. 76 in the book The Historic Henry Rifle as having been issued to the 3rd Regiment U.S. Veteran Volunteers. A letter from Springfield Research service disclosed that this rifle is listed in the company and regimental books of the 3rd U.S. Veteran Volunteer Infantry in the National Archives and that it was issued to Pvt. Michael Link of Company B, 3rd U.S. Veteran Volunteers. This unit was organized in February and March of 1865 with the intended purpose of becoming an elite corps of shock troops under Gen. Hancock. However, in April 1865 when Gen. Robert E. Lee surrendered they were left with little to do except garrison duty in the defense of Washington. The unit was mustered out of service on July 20, 1866. As part of their enlistment bonus they were allowed to keep their arms and accoutrements upon discharge. **$34,500**

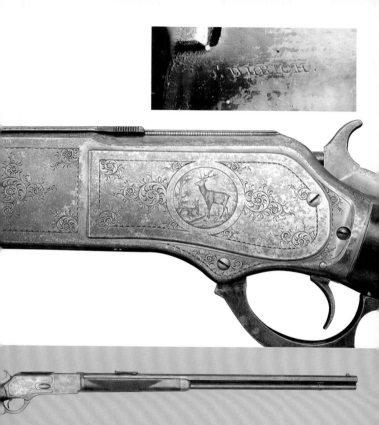

Cased Engraved Winchester Model 1866 Lever Action Rifle

This .44 Henry rimfire, SN 46027, is an extraordinary rifle in exceptionally fine condition worthy of the highest level of collector. The rifle, which is beautifully engraved by master engraver L.D. Nimschke, has a 24-1/4" octagon barrel, full magazine, 1/2-nickel front sight and Henry-style ladder rear sight, and Winchester and King's patent markings on the top flat. It is mounted with highly figured American walnut stock and forearm, uncheckered with straight grip and crescent ▶

▶ buttplate with trap containing a four-piece brass and iron-wiping rod. The receiver, forend cap and buttplate are silver plated while the lever, hammer and trigger are gold washed. The rifle comes with its original Schuyler, Harley and Graham rosewood case, measuring 46-1/2" long, 10-5/8" wide and 3" deep. The case is lined with red and green velvet, French fitted with compartments for the rifle and 10 full boxes of original .44 rimfire ammunition with a covered compartment in the right

rear and a mahogany cartridge block in the front containing 41 rounds of raised "H" Winchester ammunition. According to family history this rifle was presented to James J. Hill. Hill, who is credited with building the Great Northern Railroad and, along with J. Pierpont Morgan, also acquired the Northern Pacific and the Burlington lines. He was also a steamboat magnate and ran a shipping line from the Columbia River down to San Francisco and to the Orient. **$224,250**

Winchester Deluxe Model 1866 Rifle

A rare example of a deluxe, factory panel scene engraved, Winchester Model 1866 rifle that was manufactured in 1870. This Third Model 1866 rifle, SN79860, has the distinctive receiver profile and serial number stamped on the lower tang. The full octagon barrel has a dovetail mounted front sight with nickel-silver blade and Henry style folding leaf rear sight. The magazine has a threaded cap. The top barrel flat is roll-stamped with the second style legend "WINCHESTER'S-REPEATING ARMS. NEW HAVEN. CT. KING'S-IMPROVEMENT-PATENTED-MARCH 29. 1866. OCTOBER 16. 1860" in two lines ahead of the rear sight. The serial number is stamped on the lower tang behind the trigger and surrounded by an engraved banner. The barrel and magazine are blued, the hammer and lever are color case hardened and the brass forearm cap, receiver and buttplate are gold plated. The stock and forearm are highly figured, fancy grade walnut. The forearm cap, receiver and buttplate are factory engraved with semi-relief Germanic scrollwork on a punch-dot background that includes a partially concealed hound, buffalo and grizzly bear. The sides of the receiver are engraved with highly detailed and unique customer requested scenes. Conrad F. Ulrich engraved the rifle. **$103,500**

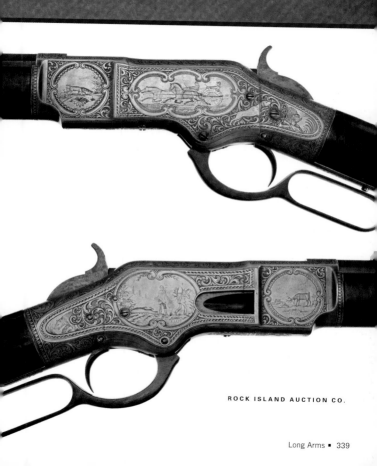

Winchester Deluxe Model 1866 Rifle

This Deluxe Third Model Winchester Rifle, SN 79868, .44 rimfire, was manufactured in 1870 and factory engraved and signed by Master Engraver Conrad F. Ulrich (rear of the trigger and numerous times on the face of receiver under forearm) and features a gold-plated brass receiver, forearm cap and crescent buttplate, 24" blue octagon barrel and full length magazine and casehardened hammer and lever. The stock and forearm are highly figured fancy grain walnut. The barrel has a dovetail mounted sporting front sight with nickel-silver blade and an early Henry-style folding leaf rear sight with rounded top and 900-yard center notch.

ROCK ISLAND AUCTION CO.

The top barrel flat is roll-stamped with the two-line legend "WINCHESTER'S-REPEATING ARMS. NEW HAVEN CT./KING'S -IMPROVEMENT- PATENTED MARCH 29. 1866. OCTOBER 16 1860". The engraver's signature "C.F. ULRICH" with a rectangular border is stamped in tiny letters on the lower tang immediately behind the trigger. Additional "C.F. ULRICH" stampings are found on the side of the upper tang under the stock and on the breech face of the receiver. "OXX" is stamped on the lower tang under the stock. The rifle has Winchester Style One factory engraving and the receiver has extensive intricate scroll engraving with two scenes on either side of the receiver and several animals and figures partially concealed in the delicate scrollwork. This rifle represents some of Conrad F. Ulrich's most detailed and best-known engraving. **$57,500**

This scarce example of a factory engraved Model 1866, SN
38583, was manufactured in 1869. Accompanied by a letter from
author and firearms expert R.L. Wilson: "The model 1866 lever
action was the first of the company's products not only to carry the
Winchester name, but to excel in the profusion of embellishments,
and the quality and quantity of decorated arms." Master engraver
John Ulrich is credited with engraving this rifle. The engraving
features bold Germanic scrollwork on a fine punch-dot background
and has a duck and a hound's head in panels on the right side of

Engraved Winchester Model 1866 Rifle

the frame and a bear's head and an inscription plate on the left side of the frame. A wolf's head is engraved in the scrollwork on the right side of the frame below the hammer. The rifle has a 24" octagon barrel, full-length magazine with brass forearm cap, frame and crescent buttplate. The barrel has a dovetail mounted sporting style front sight with nickel-silver blade and a Henry style folding leaf rear sight with 900-yard center notch. Factory sling swivels are mounted on the forearm cap and stock. The stock and forearm are walnut with a varnished finish. **$80,500**

Very fine .44 Henry rimfire standard rifle, SN 38369, with 24-1/4" octagon barrel, full magazine, half nickel front sight and 900-yard Henry-style ladder rear sight. Top flat of barrel has Winchester and King's patent markings. Mounted with uncheckered straight grain American walnut with straight stock and crescent brass buttplate with trap containing an original four-piece brass and steel cleaning rod. Top tang channel of the buttstock and inside toe of buttplate are marked with the last four digits of serial number. The '66 is the repeating rifle most deserving of the name "The Gun That Won The West," according to *Flayderman's Guide to Antique American Firearms*. **$25,875**

Winchester
Model 1866
Lever Action Rifle

PHOTO COURTESY JAMES D. JULIA, INC.

Winchester Model 1873
First Model Saddle Ring Carbine

PHOTO COURTESY JAMES D. JULIA, INC.

The Model 1873 was one of the most popular lever actions Winchester ever produced. This is "the gun that won the West." This 1873, SN 15354, .44 WCF (44-40), is a standard grade carbine, First Model, second type with mortised, impressed thumb print dust cover. It has 20" barrel and full magazine with integral front band/front sight and Model 1866 style two-position flip rear sight graduated to 500 yards. Receiver has a staple and ring in the left side. Mounted with uncheckered, slab sawed American walnut. The Model 1873 was the first centerfire carbine introduced and was enormously popular on the American frontier serving in adverse conditions with little or no maintenance, usually in a saddle scabbard, wagon or stagecoach etc. Winchester Firearms Factory letter identifies gun was received in warehouse on March 15, 1878, shipped from warehouse on May 30, 1878. CONDITION: Extremely Fine. **$22,425**

"One of One Thousand" Winchester Model 1873

This is an exceptional, totally original Winchester First Model 1873 "One of One Thousand" rifle, which author and historian R.L. Wilson calls "legends of American rifle making." In terms of rarity and desirability, original "1 of 1000" rifles rank among the most desired of all collectible firearms. A Cody Firearms Museum letter states the rifle, SN 18267, was shipped from the Winchester warehouse on May 6, 1878, and describes the rifle as "1 of 1000" with case hardened finish, "1/2 Octagon" barrel, set trigger and "XXXX Checkered stock". Even amongst "1 of 1000s" this rifle stands out as one of the finest and rarest examples. Winchester only produced 133 "1 of 1000 rifles", of those 133 only seven were manufactured with a half octagon barrel, five with 24" barrel and two with 26" barrel. Only 14 of the 133 were furnished with XXXX wood, and only five featured a short magazine. This rifle is the only one manufactured in this configuration. The barrel has the Fourth Style markings that consist of "One of One Thousand" engraved in script on top of the barrel flat between the rear sight and the frame. The legend is enclosed in an oval panel with scalloped borders and an engraved flourish next to the rear sight. The sides of the barrel below the inscription are decorated with engraved scrollwork on a punch-dot background. The muzzle has the same engraved scrollwork as the area below the legend. The barrel is blued and the forearm tip, frame, lever, hammer and crescent steel buttplate have a color casehardened finish. The stock and forearm are deluxe fancy grain XXXX checkered walnut with a high polish varnish finish. The half-round/half octagon barrel has a standard, sporting style front sight with nickel-silver blade and a sporting rear sight with serrated edges. The rifle has the first style frame with dust cover guides on the upper front sides and dust cover with oval 5/8" thumbprint. **$402,500**

Deluxe Winchester 1st Model 1873 Lever Action Rifle

This scarce late 1st Model Winchester, SN16140, is a deluxe special order rifle with 24-1/4" round barrel, button magazine, half-nickel front sight and short semi-buckhorn rear sight with serrated edges. Serials numbers for the late 1st Model 1873 range around 1600 to 31000. Deluxe 1st model 1873s are in short supply, and locating one with high original finish is a great find. To the good fortune of collectors, Winchester Museum factory records are virtually complete for the Model 1873, making it a model a collector can specialize in. This rifle was received in the warehouse April 19, 1876 and shipped April 2, 1878.

$57,500

Engraved
Winchester
Model 1873
Saddle Ring
Carbine

Spectacular full nickel engraved 1873 carbine, SN 93927, .44 WCF (44-40) with 20" barrel, full magazine, barleycorn front sight and reverse mounted, original "1873" marked carbine ladder rear sight. Mounted with uncheckered, about 2-3X, American walnut with standard carbine forearm and straight stock and carbine buttplate with trap which contains an original three-piece brass and iron cleaning rod. Receiver is beautifully engraved by John Ulrich and signed on bottom tang. Engraving consists of the vignette of a grizzly bear on the left sideplate and a bugling elk on right side, all surrounded by wonderful intertwined foliate arabesque patterns with a large flower blossom also on left side. Accompanied by a Cody Firearms Museum letter identifying this carbine as received in warehouse June 10, 1882 and shipped same day. Engraved 1873 carbines are very rare; nickel finish ones even more rare; and highly figured wood without checkering is the most rare. Usually the arms of this era saw hard service on the American frontier with very little or no maintenance and are rarely found with high original finish. **$63,250**

Presentation Factory-Engraved Winchester Model 1873

This beautiful John Ulrich engraved Model 1873, SN 148025, .44 WCF (44-40), has a 24-1/4" octagon barrel, full magazine, wind gage globe front sight, semi-buckhorn rear sight and a thin base Vernier tang sight with 3" staff. Mounted with extraordinary 3-4X American walnut with H-style checkered forearm and serpentine pistol grip stock with black fleur-de-lis insert and full-checkered hard rubber buttplate. Left side plate has the large oval panel inscribed in period script and block letters "Presented to / GEORGE P. BISSELL / Colonel 25th Reg.t C.V. / by members of the Regiment / as a slight testimonial of affection / for their old Commander". Left front flat is engraved with the vignette of the 19th Corps badge of the Civil War. Col. George Bissell was the commander of the 25th Regiment, Connecticut Volunteers, a nine-month regiment recruited in the fall of 1862 and mustered into service on Nov. 11, 1862. **$94,875**

Winchester 3rd Model
1876 Lever Action Rifle

$69,000

This beautiful and rare special-order deluxe Model 1876, SN 45720, .45-60 caliber, has a 30" full-matted octagon barrel, full magazine, blued Rocky Mountain front sight, "1876" marked ladder rear sight and a Lyman tang sight. The caliber marking is on the right top flat of the barrel over chamber area instead of the left top flat as is usually found. Mounted with about 2-3X beautiful burl and shell grain American walnut with H-style

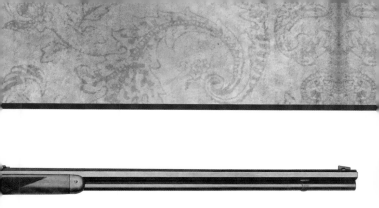

checkered forearm and serpentine grip buttstock with fleur-de-lis inlay and smooth blued steel buttplate. Accompanied by a Cody Firearms Museum letter, which identifies this rifle received in warehouse July 24, 1885 and shipped same day. Only a few more than 63,000 Model 1876s were produced in the period 1876-98 and of those very few had extra length barrels. Deluxe rifles with this feature are exceedingly rare. **$69,000**

Winchester Model 1876
Lever Action Rifle

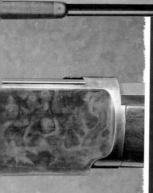

The Model 1876 was manufactured c. 1876-1897 with a total production of 63,871. Often called the "Centennial Model" because of its introduction in 1876, the rifle was designed to offer the shooter a large caliber lever action for big game. This exceptionally fine example, SN 52111, is a .40-60 caliber with a 28" octagon barrel, full magazine, blued Rocky Mountain front sight and "1876" marked ladder rear sight. Receiver, forend cap and buttplate are color case hardened. Mounted with nicely figured, uncheckered American walnut with straight stock and crescent buttplate with trap containing an original five-piece brass and steel cleaning rod. Accompanied by a Cody Firearms Museum letter which identifies this rifle, as found, received in warehouse April 21, 1886. **$48,875**

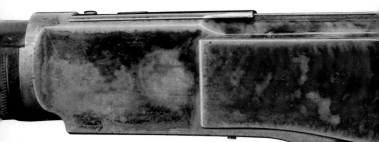

Winchester 2nd Model
1876 Deluxe Sporting Rifle

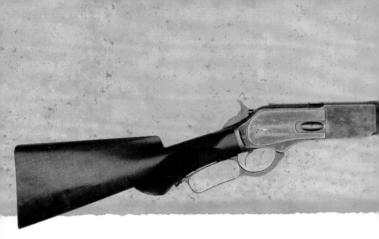

This scarce Model 1876, SN 9784, .50 Express (50-95), comes blue and color case hardened with 22" round barrel, button magazine, half nickel front sight and early short semi-buckhorn rear sight with checkered edges. Caliber marking is engraved over chamber area and left side of chamber area, and frame has British proofs. This was undoubtedly a British sportsman's India tiger rifle or African rifle. Accompanied by a Winchester Firearms Factory letter identifying rifle received in warehouse on November 18, 1879, shipped from warehouse on November

19, 1879. Top of receiver has an attached rail with second type dust cover that has impressed thumbprint and is engraved "WINCHESTER EXPRESS / .50 CAL 95 GRS". Mounted with extra finish, very nicely figured, early style checkered American walnut with pistol grip stock having a black fleur-de-lis inlay in grip cap and a smooth steel buttplate. Left side of lower tang, under the wood, is marked with the assembly number "734" and "X". The assembly number is also found in the top tang channel of the buttstock along with a "P". **$46,020**

Winchester Model 1876
Open Top Saddle Ring Carbine

This rare Model 1876, SN 2737, .45-75 caliber, standard grade carbine with 22" round barrel, has a square base barleycorn front sight with 2-position early flip rear sight graduated to 500 yards. Receiver is without dust cover, open top style with a stud and ring in left side.

Mounted with uncheckered straight grain American walnut with full length forearm that has metal forend cap and a single barrel band. Stock has a straight grip with smooth steel carbine/musket style buttplate. This second-year production carbine, quite unusually, remains in outstanding original condition contrary to those of this era which are usually hard used and without original finish. Very fine condition. Barrel retains 95-97% strong original blue with slight muzzle edge wear and a couple of small spots of discoloration. Receiver retains 60-70% strong original blue with balance flaked, not worn, to a blue/brown patina. Sideplates retain 75-80% strong original blue mixed with flaking. Hammer retains most of its strong original case colors, lightly faded. Wood is sound with very minor handling and use nicks and scratches and retains virtually all of its original oil finish. Mechanics are crisp, bright shiny bore. **$21,240**

Special Order Engraved
Winchester Model 1886

A wonderful deluxe Model 1886, SN 6928, .45-90 caliber with 26" round barrel, button magazine, Rocky Mountain front sight and altered semi-buckhorn rear sight. Receiver engraved by John Ulrich, signed on bottom tang, in style #10 with a #7 bull moose vignette on left side. Right side is engraved in a panel above loading gate "E.B.M. FROM A.W.H." Sides of lever and hammer, forend cap, top and bottom tangs and bolt are engraved to match. Engraving extends over chamber area of barrel and around front sight. Chamber end of barrel and muzzle have silver band inlays. Mounted with spectacular, streaky, burl walnut with H-style checkered forearm and straight stock with Winchester hard rubber buttplate. Cody Firearms Museum letter identifies this rifle received in warehouse Aug. 4, 1887. **$74,750**

Extremely rare engraved and gold inlaid Model 1886, SN 99580, 45-70 caliber, with 26" octagon to round barrel, 2/3 magazine, ivory bead hunting front sight, slot blank in rear seat and Lyman tang sight. Receiver is factory engraved probably by John Ulrich, in a modified #10 style with a large panel on left side inlaid in gold script "Winchester / Repeating Arms Co. / 1895." all surrounded by gold wire inlay. Right side has the vignette of a bugling bull elk. Mounted with 3-4X, extremely beautiful flame and shell grain American walnut with H-style checkered forearm and serpentine grip with black insert and Winchester hard rubber buttplate. Accompanied by a Cody Firearms Museum letter, which identifies this rifle received in warehouse May 23, 1895, and shipped same day. This rifle is pictured on p. 227 of The Book of Winchester Engraving, Wilson, and on p. 240 of Winchester Engraving, Wilson, with credit to the Ivan B. Hart Collection. Wilson notes that "It is likely the rifle was used as a sample or show gun." **$40,250**

Winchester Model 1886 "Show" Rifle

Winchester Model 1886
Lever Action Rifle

This rare, inscribed, deluxe engraved Model 1886, SN 24468, .45-90 caliber features a 26" octagon barrel, full magazine, half nickel front sight, semi-buckhorn rear sight, Lyman tang sight and ingle set trigger. Receiver has $4.00 engraved in #10-style consisting of a standing whitetail buck on left side and the inscription on the right side "Made Expressly For William Ross Tulloch" surrounded by light foliate arabesque patterns. Forend cap and buttplate tang are engraved to match. Mounted with very highly figured marbled and flame grain American walnut with H-style checkered forearm and serpentine grip stock with black insert, cheekpiece and nickeled brass Swiss buttplate. The Model 1886 was manufactured c. 1888-1935 with a total production run of 159,994. Made in a variety of calipers from as small as .33 W.C.F. to as large as .50-110 Express. This example retains virtually all of its factory restored finish to both metal and wood with brilliant case colors, lightly faded outer faces of lever, crisp bright blue and piano type varnish finish. Mechanics are crisp, bright shiny bore. **$31,625**

Special-Order Winchester Model 1886

This beautiful Model 1886 rifle, SN 97046, is a .45-90 caliber with a rare 30" octagon barrel, full magazine, globe front sight, slot blank in rear seat and a Lyman tang sight. Mounted with uncheckered straight grain American walnut with buttstock that has serpentine grip with black insert and crescent buttplate. Buttstock and forend cap have sling eyes. Receiver has single set trigger. Accompanied by a Cody Firearms Museum letter identifying this rifle, as found, received in warehouse Feb. 14, 1895. The rifle appears to be in new and unfired condition. **$50,600**

Factory Engraved Winchester Model 1886

Based on a John Browning patent, the Model 1886 was one of the finest and strongest lever actions ever utilized in a Winchester rifle. The Model 1886 was produced from 1886 to 1935 with about 160,000 in production. In 1901 Winchester discontinued the use of case hardened frames on all rifles and used blued frames instead. For this reason, case hardened Model 1886 rifles such as this one bring a premium from collectors. This deluxe Model 1886, SN 99572, .45-90 W.C.F., comes with 26" octagon barrel, full magazine, ivory bead Lyman front sight and Marbles folding rear sight with a Lyman large loop tang sight. Receiver and forend cap are color case hardened and engraved in No. 10 style. Engraving consists of the large vignette of a standing whitetail buck in a mountain scene surrounded by a large counterpoint circle with foliate arabesque patterns front and back and a double line border. Right side is lightly engraved in matching foliate arabesque patterns and borders. Rifle is mounted with beautiful XXX center crotch, flame grain burl walnut with matching forearm, checkered in "H" style with serpentine pistol grip that has a black insert and a Winchester hard rubber buttplate. A Winchester Firearms Factory letter and a Cody Firearms Museum fact sheet identifies this rifle as received in the warehouse on 2 May 1895 and shipped on 13 May 1895. **$63,250**

Semi-Deluxe "Big 50" Winchester Model 1886

A rare, special-order Model 1866, SN 158359, .50-110 caliber, with 26" octagon to round barrel. Features scarce full magazine, takedown with Sheard front sight, platinum line rear sight and Lyman tang sight. Mounted with nicely figured, slab sawed American walnut with I-style checkered forearm and capped pistol grip stock with Winchester hard rubber buttplate. This rifle was produced in 1921 near the very end of 1886 production and the caliber is unusual in this late configuration. Extremely fine condition. **$27,600**

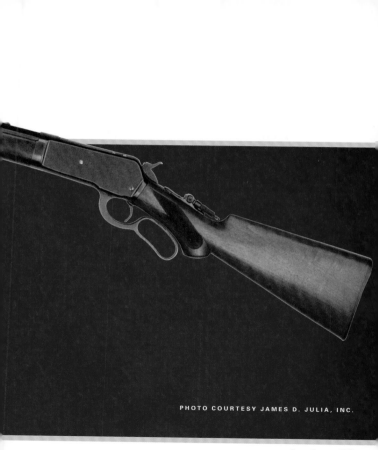

Winchester Model 1886, Scare Caliber

This Model 1886, SN 95835, is a .40-70 caliber standard grade rifle with 26" octagon barrel, full magazine, half nickel front sight, Lyman 6A two-leaf folding rear sight and Lyman tang sight. Mounted with uncheckered straight grain American walnut with straight stock and crescent buttplate. Accompanied by a Cody Firearms Museum letter identifying it as received in warehouse Feb. 6, 1895 and shipped May 11, 1895. This cartridge was introduced for the 1886 in 1894 but was not much of an improvement over the 38-55 cartridge being chambered in the much lighter Model 1894 rifle and drew little interest from consumers. **$25,300**

Deluxe Engraved Winchester Model 1894

This is a spectacular, deluxe panel scene Ulrich Factory engraved gold inlaid Winchester Model 1894 Fancy Sporting Rifle, manufactured in 1901. The rifle, SN 266180, was engraved by master Winchester engraver John Ulrich and signed "J. ULRICH" in tiny letters on the lower tang behind the trigger. This rifle features deluxe Winchester "No. 4 Engraving" and "Style D" carving and checkering on the stock and forearm. The left side of the receiver is engraved with a highly detailed game scene that depicts a hunter taking two elk. The right side of the receiver is engraved with a solitary grizzly bear. The receiver, loading lever link, takedown collar, barrel, forearm cap and buttplate heel are inlaid with gold bands and borders. The loading lever, hammer and screw heads are all engraved. This rifle has a blue finish on the barrel, magazine, forearm cap and receiver. The loading lever, hammer and crescent buttplate have a color case hardened finish. The loading gate is niter blued. The highly figured carved walnut pistol grip stock and forearm have a high polish "piano" finish. The pistol grip has a black, hard rubber cap embossed "WINCHESTER REPEATING ARMS". The barrel is fitted with a dove-tail mounted, gold washed, Beach or Lyman folding combination front sight and a scarce Winchester tangent style rear sight for Model 1894 rifles chambered for high velocity, smokeless, cartridges. **$115,000**

The Model 1894 Winchester was first manufactured c. 1894 and evolved into the company's most successful selling centerfire rifle. This is an extremely rare first Model 1894, SN 46, .38-45 caliber carbine with 20" barrel, full magazine, German silver front sight, carbine ladder rear sight and a staple and ring in left side of receiver. Mounted with uncheckered, nicely figured, slab sawed American walnut with straight stock and carbine buttplate. Carbines in this configuration are extraordinarily rare. Rifle is in very fine to extremely fine condition. **$63,250**

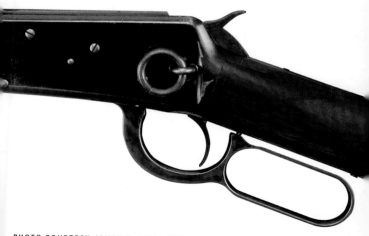

Winchester First Model 1894 Saddle Ring Carbine

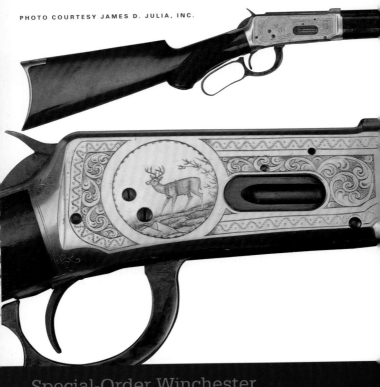

Special-Order Winchester
Model 1894 Short Rifle

An extraordinarily rare example of a special-order, factory-engraved Model 1894, SN 64062, .30 caliber W.C.F. (30-30). According to the Cody Firearms Museum, Buffalo Bill Historical Center, Cody, Wyoming, regarding the production of the Winchester Model 1894 in the serial range "1 through 353,999" there were only 22 arms produced with non-standard wood and this rifle is the only one produced with mahogany. Additionally, there were only 2,252 produced with 22" barrels and only 336 rifles were engraved. There were only 56 gold-plated or trimmed guns. This rifle has a 22" octagon barrel, full magazine, Lyman ivory bead front sight with screw and a 3-leaf platinum line express rear sight. Mounted with fine-grained mahogany wood with H-style checkered 8-3/8" forearm and capped pistol grip stock with crescent buttplate. Receiver, forend cap, magazine band and buttplate are heavily gold plated. Receiver is factory engraved in style #9 with the vignettes of a running whitetail buck on left side surmounted by the script name "I.M. Lawrence" and the right side has a standing whitetail buck. Rifle manufactured in 1896. Very fine condition. **$63,250**

Winchester Model 1894 Presentation Rifle

Extremely rare presentation engraved, gold-plated takedown, special-order Model 1894 lever action rifle, SN 384777, .25-35 caliber with 24-1/4" octagon to round barrel, half magazine, takedown, globe front sight, folding leaf rear sight and locking Lyman tang sight. Receiver, forend cap and buttplate are gold plated and has close-coupled double-set triggers. Receiver is engraved in style #4 by John Ulrich and signed on bottom tang just behind the trigger slot. Left side of receiver has the fabulous full vignette of a hunter shooting from behind a tree with two bull elk in the foreground. Right side, in place of the usual style #4 bear vignette, is inscribed in period script "Presented to / George Rutledge / by / R.M. Dudley / January 1st / 1912". Both sides are surrounded by foliate arabesque scrolls with very fine shaded background. **$57,500**

Presented to
George Rutledge
by
R. M. Landley
January 1st
1912

J. T......CH

Winchester "Big 50" Lever Action Rifle

This standard grade lever action rifle, SN 134578, .50 Ex (50-110) features a 26" octagon barrel, full magazine, Lyman ivory bead front sight, rear sight altered to flat top and a Lyman loop tang sight. Barrel is marked "NICKEL STEEL" on top left flat by rear sight. Accompanied by a Cody Firearms Museum research request identifying rifle in caliber 50 Express, octagon (nickel steel) barrel, plain trigger, Lyman front and sporting rear sights and "TARGET FOR 100 YDS W.H.V. (WITH HIGH VELOCITY AMMUNITION)". It was received in warehouse June 27, 1905. This rifle is unusual with its crescent buttplate as this huge caliber with severe recoil was very uncomfortable to shoot with anything but a shotgun buttplate. CONDITION: Extremely Fine Plus. **$28,175**

PHOTO COURTESY JAMES D. JULIA, INC.

Winchester Model 20
Junior Trap Shooting Outfit

The Model 20, SN 9945, .410 with 26" barrel with full choke, was a trim small bore shotgun offered 1920-1924. It featured a blued finish with Schnabel forearm and pistol grip stock of standard black walnut. The gun was also offered in a set known as the Winchester Junior Trap Shooting Outfit and promoted as a family shooting game. The black leatherette case (30"x 8-3/4" x 6") contains a Winchester midget hand trap and steel two-piece cleaning rod; 2-oz tube of Winchester gun grease in green box; Winchester gun oil; Winchester rust remover; and a case of 100 midget sized clay targets. The shotgun shells are marked "410 (12 m/m)" and contained 25 2" shells with number 8 shot. These shells have a distinctive black label and were available only with the junior trap shooting outfit making them extremely scarce today. Paperwork with the set includes: Winchester general instruction booklet, "A Whole New Field of Sport" booklet, use and care booklet and packet of score sheets. **$12,075**

Rare Winchester
Model 55
Deluxe Rifle

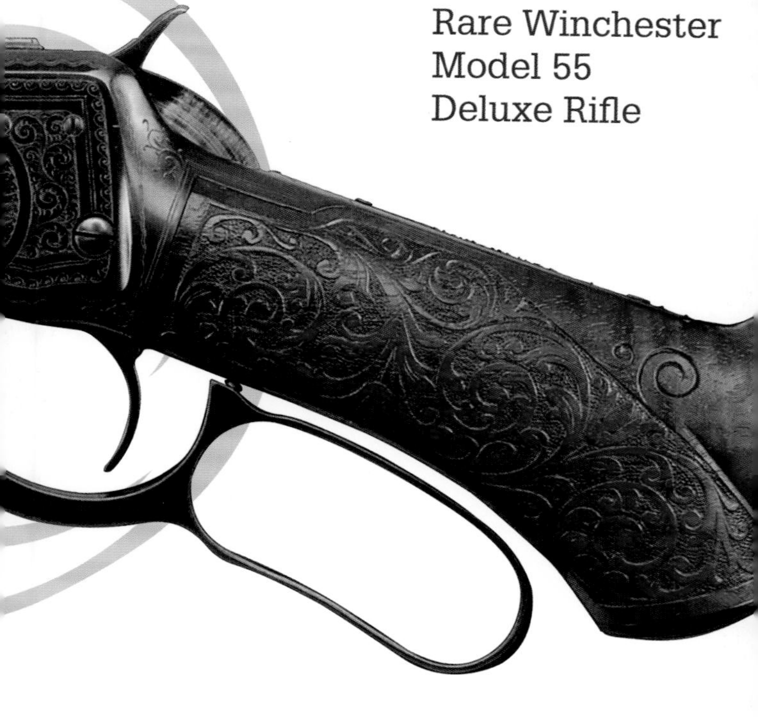

The Model 55 was manufactured from 1924 to 1932. This extremely rare example, SN 1817, .30 WCF. (30-30) is one of only a few known and may be the only one of its configuration. Rifle has a 24-1/4" lightweight tapered round barrel, half magazine, takedown with gold bead pedestal front sight and semi-buckhorn rear sight. Receiver is factory engraved in a slightly modified #2 pattern consisting of a standing whitetail buck and doe in a mountain meadow on the left side and a walking bull moose on right side. **$23,575**

Winchester
Model 21

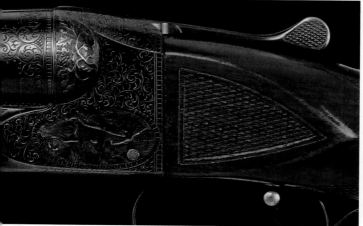

The Model 21 was Winchester's finest effort with regard to quality, reliability and strength. Despite the Model 21 being offered as a production gun it was, in fact, a hand-built custom-made shotgun. The gun was introduced in 1931. From 1931-1959 about 30,000 guns were sold. This splendid engraved pre-WWII shotgun, SN 8218, (1935), .12 gauge with 30" barrels was most liked engraved by master Winchester engraver Alden George Ulrich. The gun was built for Col. W. F. Siegmund, a Winchester/Olin executive. The gun is a very fine example of Winchester's elite pre-war custom work. **$19,550**

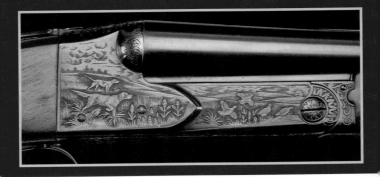

Custom
Engraved
Winchester
Model 21

This engraved .20 gauge for skeet, SN 10983, 26" barrels with second type markings on left side, in use briefly during the mid 1930s, has Winchester "WS-1" and "WS-2" on bottoms. Buttstock with unusual round knob pistol grip, has standard pattern checkering, and measures 14" over skeet type checkered wood butt and is numbered to the gun. Weight: 6 lbs. 6 oz. Action is engraved with exceptionally well cut scenes of feathered game and dogs in the style of, and probably the work of, Rudolf Kornbrath, but may be the work of his protégée, Josef Fugger. Left side of action portrays a trio of flushing pheasants on edge of meadow at front, with pair of setters toward rear of action. Foreground is nicely detailed with grass and sedge. Right side has covey of quail in rolling prairie, with setter pointing and pointer honoring point toward rear. Bottom of action has trio of ruffed grouse flying through tree branches with bemused pointer at bottom looking on. A pair of woodcock flitting through alders is on trigger guard bow. **$21,850**

Winchester-Hotchkiss
Second Model Bolt Action

TWENTY
RIFLE CARTRIDGES,
2".4 Case, 80 Grain Charge, 500 Grain Bullet.
MANUFACTURED AT THE FRANKFORD ARSENAL.

GENERAL DIRECTIONS FOR RELOADING.

After every fire, extract primers, and wash cases in hot water; wipe them dry; lubricate body
slightly, keeping interior of shell and pocket free from grease; and in the order named, resize,
prime, (preferably by pressure,) load and crimp.   After resizing, remove burrs of the mouth
with the scraper.

PRECAUTIONS.

Inspect all fired shells, and reject defective or doubtful ones.   Resize shells after every round.
Before using, lubricate the WHOLE cartridge wall, using grease or oil free from salt or acid.

☞   Never attempt to prime a loaded shell.

This rare U.S. Department of Indian Affairs Saddle Ring Carbine, SN 16214, .45-70 caliber, has a 24" inch barrel with standard sights, single barrel band and marked near breech: Co. D. Blued finish. Case hardened bolt action. Straight bolt toggle. Saddle ring. Varnished walnut stock, the left side marked: USDIA [U.S. Department of Indian Affairs]. Top of buttstock marked: 10. Steel buttplate. Made in 1882. One of 4,396 manufactured. Condition: Very Good. **$2,760**

Winchester Model 1897 Double-W Cartridge Board

Beautiful and best known of the Winchester cartridge boards, this fine board, SN 191, has 182 metallic cartridges with 15 different bullets, 11 paper shot shells, 9 brass shot shells and 9 round glass-top tins of primers and percussion caps. Exposed image size is about 49" x 31-3/4" in its original gold, gesso lined oak frame measuring about 57-1/2" x 40-1/4". All of the cartridges and cap boxes are individually labeled. **$25,300**

Browning Superposed
Grade IV-W.410

This Browning over/under, SN P83RN1064, .410-gauge has 26-1/2" Barrels with raised, ventilated rib, choked IC and modified. Grey sideplated action is engraved with semi-relief large shaded scroll and acanthus, having strap work highlights as background for semi-relief gold inlaid game birds. Pheasants and quail are on left sideplate; four ducks in marsh are on right; flying quail is on bottom of action; and dogs head is on trigger guard bow. Each sideplate is signed by engraver, "J. Lewanczyk". Very fine, flame, stump figured straight grip, oil finished buttstock features checkered wood butt and curved border checkering. Weight: 6 lbs. 9 oz. CONDITION: Excellent. **$29,900**

Browning Superposed Midas Grade

PHOTO COURTESY JAMES D. JULIA, INC.

The Superposed Shotgun series was introduced in 1930 and is manufactured by Fabrique Nationale in Belgium. This 1966 Midas Grade, SN 1564J6, comes with .410/ .20 gauge/ and .28 gauge 28" barrels with raised ventilated ribs and standard markings are marked "1", "2", and "3" and all are stamped "**S" on left sides of breech ends. Blued action with nicely cut large open scrolled acanthus with delicate stippled shading, has Vranken inspired gold inlays; a trio of pheasants on left side of action, ducks on right, and quail on bottom. Engravers signature "J. Lodewyc" is on bottom rear of each side of action. Nicely crotch figured American walnut round knob buttstock measures 14-5/8". Wraparound checkering is of modified point pattern with flourish at rear, and has beaded border. Matching semi-beavertail forends have point pattern checkering. BARREL set no. "1" .410: Bore diameter at muzzle: top -.405, bottom -.405. Wall thickness: top -.050, bottom -.044. Drop at heel: 2-3/16", drop at comb: 1-17/32". Weight: 7 lbs. 3 oz, LOP 14-5/8". BARREL set no. "2" 20 gauge: Bore diameter: top -.619, bottom -.619. Bore restrictions: top -.003, bottom -.003. Wall thickness: top -.042, bottom -.045. Drop at heel: 2-1/8", drop at comb: 1-1/2". Weight: 6 lbs. 15 oz, LOP 14-5/8". BARREL set no. "3" 28 gauge: Bore diameter: top -.547, bottom -.542. Bore restrictions: top -.008, bottom -.002. Wall thickness: top -.040, bottom -.041. Drop at heel: 2-1/4", drop at comb: 1-1/2". Weight: 6 lbs. 14 oz, LOP 14-5/8". Tan vinyl Browning case with light tan faux fur interior contains guarantee card and two keys. **$23,000**

Browning .20-Gauge Custom Exhibition Superlight

This shotgun, SN 3368V73, .20 gauge, 2-3/4" Chambers comes with 26-3/8" barrels with Morgan, Utah and Montreal address fitted with narrow, ventilated rib and marked for skeet. Typical action, blued in Midas style, is very finely engraved with well cut open shaded scroll and acanthus, framing vignettes of dogs and game gold inlaid in semi-relief, outlined by gold wire inlaid borders. Left side of action depicts setter pointing pair of departing partridge with mountains and trees in background; pointer pointing pair of grouse in open woodland is on right; bottom of action has large shaded scroll with gold wire outlined to barrel lugs and cocking lever. Trigger plate is engraved "Engraved by" "C Hunt Turner". Boldly flame figured, nicely streaked Claro walnut straight grip modified point pattern checkered buttstock measures 14-1/4" over Browning composition buttplate. **$15,525**

Colt Model 1855
British Carbine

Fine British carbine, SN 11999, .56 caliber with 21" octagon to round barrel, brass front sight and military style 3-leaf, two folding, one standing rear sight graduated 100, 300 and 500 yards. Top strap is marked "COL. COLT HARTFORD CT. U.S.A.". Left side of frame has standard patent markings and is mounted with a stud and ring. Left barrel flat and flutes of cylinder have British proofs. Stock is nicely figured American walnut with checkered wrist and brass trigger guard and buttplate. Barrel is numbered "11999". British carbines are found in the serial number range between 10000 and 12000. This may be the last British carbine made. Barrel retains about 90% strong original blue with minor nicks and scratches and light muzzle end wear; frame retains about 80% original blue with the loss areas flaked to a medium patina
CONDITION: Fine **$16,100**

Colt Double Barrel Rifle

One of the great rarities of Colt collecting, about 35 Colt Double Barrel Rifles were made from 1879-1885. One of the ultra-rarities in Colts, the Double Rifle was, according to *Flayderman's Guide to Antique American Firearms*, the brainchild of Caldwell Hart Colt, the playboy son of Samuel Colt. Caldwell was an avid gun enthusiast and maintained a collection at the family home. The major share of Double Rifle production is believed to have been for Caldwell and his friends. This Double Barrel, SN 32, 45-70-caliber, has nicely browned 28" laminated Damascus barrels with full-length flat rib engraved "Colt's PT F. A. Mfg. Co. Hartford. CT. U. S. A." toward breech end. German silver blade front sight is dovetailed through ovoid base. SN is on barrel flats, and a wide sling loop is screwed to bottom rib. Lyman adjustable tang sight marked "M 84" is fitted on stock at top of grip. Case hardened action has uniquely filed fluted fences. SN is stamped on water table. Bar locks with tall serpentine flat-faced hammers are border engraved with some fine scroll and tendrils. Colt's patent "PT FA MFG. CO" is on each lockplate. There is geometric engraving on bottom of action and on blued trigger plate, which extends through to grip. SN is at grip. Very fine, nicely marbled European walnut semi-pistol grip buttstock measures 14-1/8" over steel buttplate with widow's peak. Weight: 9 lbs. 8 oz. Barrels retain 80 - 90% original brown with very fine definition to pattern. CONDITION: Very Fine. **$41,400**

Colt Model 1890 Gatling Gun

This is an excellent example of a Colt Model 1890 Gatling Gun mounted on a two-wheel carriage. This model features ten 32-inch 45-70 barrels (five inches of the muzzle end are octagon); has an overall length of 49 inches and weighs approximately 200 pounds without the carriage; and has a rate of fire of 525 rounds per minute. Essentially all models manufactured from 1889 to 1892 were identical. The breech end of each barrel is numbered 1 thru 10, proofed "V/P/eagle head" and "R.A.C." (Rinaldo A. Carr) inspected. The breech end of the breech housing is marked with the corresponding barrel number. Each barrel toward the breech end is marked with the matching assembly number, "14". ▶

▶ The top of the frame ahead of the barrels is also marked "R.A.C." and "14". The sights are mounted on the right side of the frame. The rear of the magazine feed port is marked "PATENTED/FEB. 11, 1890/R.A.C.". The top rear of the breech housing is "R.A.C." inspected over engraved "Gatling Gun/Patented/Manfd at/ COLT'S ARMORY/Hartford Conn. U.S.A./ MODEL 1890/No 505 CAL 45/SEB"(Capt. Stanhope E. Blunt). The breech end face of each bolt is marked with a "P". Inspection mark. The gun is mounted on the original iron yoke. The U.S. Army purchased 18 Model 1889 Gatling Guns (serial number 492-509), with this gun being one of those, 17 Model 1891s and 18 Model 1892s. These were the last .45-70 Gatling Guns ordered by the U.S. Government. The gun is mounted on a barracks green painted carriage with an equipment/ammunition box mounted on either side of the gun and iron banded wooden wheels. **$253,000**

THE GATLING GUN

Paul Wahl & Don Toppel

Model 1900 Colt Gatling Gun

This Model 1900 Gatling Gun, SN 1093, 30-40 Krag, comes with its original shipping crate. Usual open barrel configuration with ten 32" round to octagon barrels with brass housing and original iron rails. Top of the housing has the usual markings "GATLING GUN PATENTED / HARTFORD, CONN. U.S.A." in an elliptical shape surrounding "Manufactured By / Colt's Pt. F. A. Mfg. Co. Below that is marked "Model 1900 / Cal. 30 / No. 1093" and the inspector initials "O.C.H." (Capt. Odus C. Horney). Gun is configured for the Bruce feed housing with one original Bruce magazine. Bruce feed is marked with assembly number "13". Gun is mounted on an original brass and iron cradle and base with bright metal tiller, all of which is mounted on an original tripod base with replacement legs. One leg is stenciled "Reserve For G.A.R. Posts". Accompanied by an original iron bound wood Gatling Gun shipping crate. Barrels, frame and cradle retain about 60-80% added black paint. Brass retains a dark coffee colored patina. Tiller, crank arm and crank locking arm are bright metal. Mechanics are fine. CONDITION: Fine **$103,500**

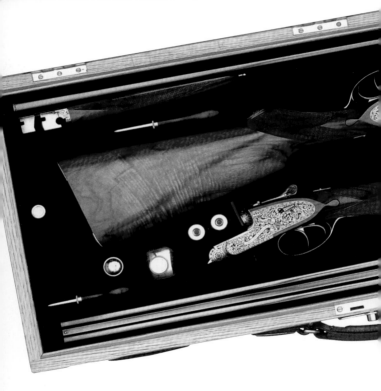

$109,250

Holland & Holland
Royal Deluxe 20
Bore Game Guns

Established in 1835, Holland & Holland has manufactured a wide variety of shotguns and rifles during its time. The greater part of these arms were made to custom order. This exceptionally fine cased-pair of guns, SN 41213/ 41214, are .20-gauge. This very fine, and unusual, pair of guns, nos. "1" and "2" inlaid in gold on breech ends of barrels, top levers, and forend tips, have finely struck 28" chopper lump barrels with medium, concave game ribs engraved "Model Deluxe". Tops of barrels are engraved "Holland and Holland 33, Bruton Street, London." Barrel flats are stamped with 1993 London proofs for 20 ga. 76mm chambers at 1200 bar. Striking, flesh-toned and dark marbled, nicely figured European walnut unusual "Prince of Wales" capped grip buttstocks measure 14-3/4" over checkered wood butts with scalloped and engraved steel heel and toe plates. CONDITION: Essentially as new, possibly unfired. $109,250

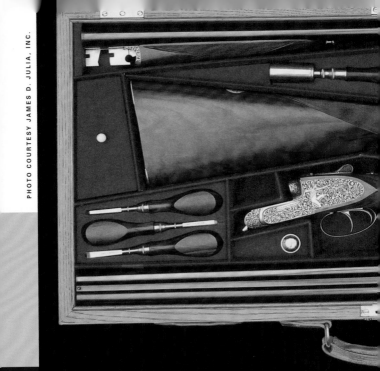

Holland & Holland Deluxe Game Guns

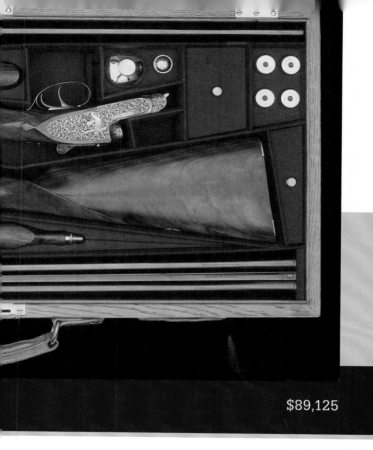

$89,125

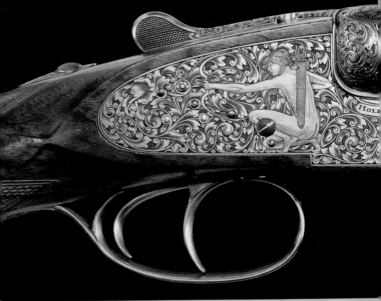

Cased pair of exceptional, Grifnee-engraved shotguns, SN 41088/ 41089, .12-gauge, with 2-3/4" Chambers. 28" Chopper lump barrels are engraved "Model Deluxe" on concave game ribs. Top of barrels are engraved "Holland and Holland 33, Bruton Street, London." Barrel flats are stamped with 1990 London nitro proofs. Actions are engraved with exceptional semi-relief large scrolled acanthus with strapwork highlights and bold background shading. Scroll of fences and top levers are in

slightly higher relief. "Holland and Holland" is in scrolled bands on each side of action. This exceptionally well done scroll is backdrop for finely detailed nude portraits of Goddess Diana in various poses with bow drawn. This exquisite work was done by noted engraver of the finest guns, the late Philippe Grifnee, whose signature is on each trigger plate. Dark marbled, flesh-toned European walnut straight grip buttstocks. CONDITION: Near new. **$89,125**

Krieghoff Model 32 Kolouch
Engraved Skeet Gun

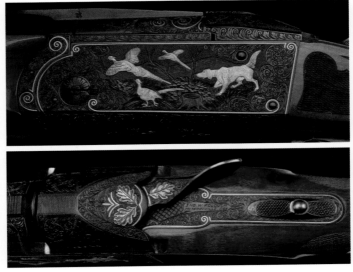

This custom gun, SN 9139, features four barrels, .12, .20, .28, and .410 gauges. This fine set with 28" ventilated rib barrels having 2" triangles of shaded open foliate scroll with gold wire scrolled inlay at breech ends, are gold inlaid with gauge on rear of rib. Typical Model 32 action with sliding top bolt, features non-automatic safety and selective single trigger. Action is heavily embellished with large open shaded foliate scroll with gold wire inlays at edges that have scrolled terminations outlining scenes of gold inlaid high relief game birds and dogs on each side; a setter is pointing trio of pheasant on left; pointer pointing trio of ruffed grouse on right; a woodcock in flight on bottom flanked by trios of white gold oak leaves; a bobwhite is flanked by single oak leaves on trigger guard bow. This work is by noted engraver, Walter Kolouch. Excellent condition. **$15,525**

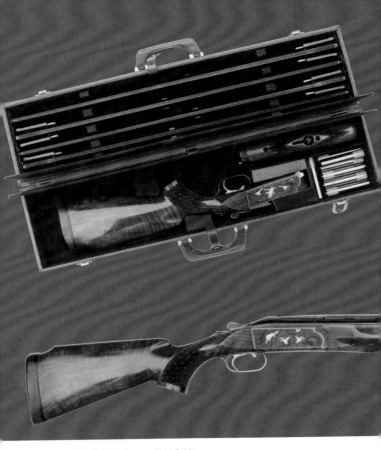

Krieghoff Model 32 Crown Grade Four Barrel Skeet Set With Case

This beautiful shotgun, SN 11814, comes with four barrels, .12, .20, .28, .410 gauges. All barrel sets are 28" with raised, ventilated ribs having ivory front and silver mid beads. All are marked "Made By H. Krieghoff Ulm - Germany" and with gauges, chambers, as well as "Bohler - Laufstahl" on left sides. Action is engraved with large foliate scroll at nearly full coverage having gold wire inlay around edges. This fine scroll frames large vignettes of relief gold inlaid game birds and predators in wooded backgrounds; an eagle is stooping on and bringing down one of a trio of flushing pheasants on left side; a fox is worrying a trio of escaping mallards on right side; bottom of action has large relief inlaid crown with "Krieghoff Model 32" flush inlaid in gold. Very Fine condition. **$15,340**

Deluxe Marlin Model 1889 Lever Action Rifle

A spectacular, gold-plated, presentation grade 1893 Chicago World's Fair Model 1889 rifle, SN 87609, .38 WCF (38-40) with 24" octagon to round barrel, half magazine, German silver Rocky Mtn. front sight and Marlin semi-buckhorn rear sight with adjustable aperture. Mounted with extremely beautiful, very highly figured, center crotch, flame grain, B-style checkered American walnut with serpentine grip and Marlin embossed hard rubber buttplate. Receiver is beautifully deep relief engraved by Conrad Ulrich in #9 style with large vignette of a standing buck deer, a standing doe and a resting doe in a very highly detailed forest scene on left side and a deep relief standing bull elk in a mountain scene on right side, all surrounded by full coverage, very fine foliate arabesque patterns with punch dot background. Right top flat of barrel is engraved in period script "Presented to H.W. Chester, by The Marlin Fire Arms Co." Left top flat of barrel is engraved in matching script "World's Fair Chicago. 1893." **$48,300**

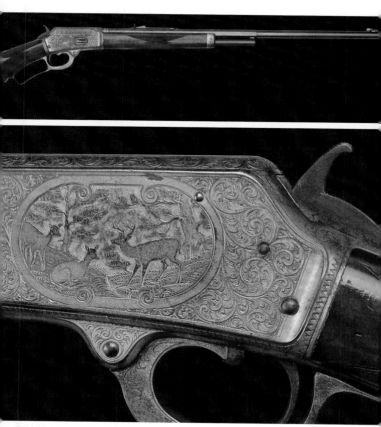

Deluxe Marlin Model 1893 Lever Action Rifle

This rare Marlin, SN 155286, 30-30, comes with 26" octagon to round barrel, full magazine, takedown with German silver Rocky Mountain front sight and sporting rear sight. Mounted with highly figured, shell grain European walnut with #10 checkered and carved forearm and serpentine pistol grip stock with Marlin hard rubber buttplate. Carving consists of a maple leaf and special borders on each side of both stock and forearm. Receiver engraved in spectacular #10 style by Conrad Ulrich. Engraving consists of the large oval vignette of a semi-relief bull moose in forest scene. Right side is engraved in a slightly smaller vignette of detailed grizzly bear in a mountain scene. Both sides of receiver have nearly full coverage, semi-relief grape leaves with fine punch dot background. Both vignettes are outlined in inlaid gold wire. While 1893 Marlin rifles are not uncommon such rifles engraved with extensive coverage with special carved wood and gold and platinum inlays, and with high original finish are exceedingly rare. Extremely Fine Plus. **$80,500**

Marlin Model 1893
Lever-Action Rifle

PHOTO COURTESY JAMES D. JULIA, INC

The Model 1893 was the first rifle Marlin designed for the then new smokeless powder cartridges. There were approximately 900,000 manufactured between 1893 and 1935. Factory records are incomplete on the 1893. This engraved special-order, SN 312535, 32-40-caliber, comes with 26" octagon to round barrel, half magazine, takedown with tall German silver Rocky Mountain front sight and semi-buckhorn rear sight. Barrel is marked "SPECIAL SMOKELESS STEEL" as are all 1893s manufactured after 1904. Top of receiver is marked "MARLIN SAFETY" with standard tang markings. Receiver, takedown ring, lever, hammer and buttplate are color case hardened with the receiver engraved in No. 1 style. Engraving is probably by Conrad Ulrich. Mounted with "A" style checkered straight grain American walnut with serpentine grip and crescent steel buttplate. A Cody Firearms Museum letter identifies rifle was shipped on Dec. 8, 1904. **$20,125**

$28,750

Annie Oakley's Special Order Parker Bros. BHE

Few evoke an association with the "Wild West" and shooting more so than "Little Sure Shot", Annie Oakley. She and her husband, Frank Butler, used many Parker shotguns during their tenure at Buffalo Bill Cody's Wild West Show, and later when they were on their own giving shooting demonstrations. ▶

► This unusual .12 gauge shotgun, SN 117432, was special ordered by Frank Butler Feb. 21, 1903, and is unique in that it is the only known Parker that actually portrays Annie. The right side of the action has Annie in her traditional shooting garb, at the ready with setter on point in circular vignette at rear, and with another smaller circular scene with two game birds, one flying and another perched in tree. Left side has Annie taking a shot with pointer in background; smaller vignette depicts one bird still flying and the other obviously shot.

These interesting scenes are surrounded by exceptionally well cut semi-relief scroll. Quality of engraving, especially scroll, is higher than that normally encountered on Parker guns. The shotgun was made without a safety, and it was ordered with dimensions very close to those that Annie was known to favor. It was supplied with Titanic steel barrels (as were many "B" grade guns), automatic ejectors, and double triggers, and was specified with 4-1/2" half pistol grip and "Silvers rubber butt". The original cost of this gun was $229. **$28,750**

Parker Bros. DHE 28 Gauge

Parker made fewer than 200 of these small bore – and very desirable – shotguns. This scarce beauty, SN 235918, matches all specifications in Parker Gun Identification and Serialization ledger, with 26" Titanic barrels, ejectors, and straight grip stock. All correct markings are on barrel flats. Nicely figured American walnut straight-grip buttstock measures 13-7/8" over skeleton steel buttplate, and features typical "D" side panels, drop points, and checkering. A silver oval on toe lines is engraved "ASI" (Austin S. Igleheart). Splinter ejector forend has typical Parker latch. Bore diameter: left -.551, right -.552. Bore restrictions: left -.023, right -.016. Wall thickness: left -.026, right -.022. Drop at heel: 2-3/4", drop at comb: 1-5/8". Weight: 5 lbs. 9 oz. **$36,225**

Purdey 100 Bore
Percussion Double Rifle

In 1852 James Purdey experimented with small caliber rifles using large powder charges, and developed a mechanically fitted conical bullet with two wings to preclude stripping across rifling. This was done to produce high velocity and long range striking energy and flat trajectory. He marketed his newly developed rifle and bullet as "The Express Train". This was later shortened and taken into everyday usage as the "Express". This rifle, SN 7044, .400-caliber, two-groove Express was sold July 5, 1865, to the famous sportsman Lord Bentinck, of whom, maker James Purdey wrote "My First and Best Customer". **$17,825**

Purdey Over-Under Sidelock
Ejector Heavy Game Gun

This very fine, single-trigger shotgun, SN 26695. (c. 1958), .12-gauge, with 26" and 28" barrels with narrow file cut ventilated ribs, are engraved "J. Purdey and Sons." and "Audley House. South Audley Street. London. England." on top. Right side of top barrel and flats of bottom barrel have London nitro proofs for 2-3/4" chambers. Action and lockplates are engraved with well executed Purdey house style rose bouquet and scroll, with "J. Purdey and Sons. London England" on bottom of action, and "J. Purdey and Sons." in scroll surrounded cartouches on lockplates. Barrels retain virtually all of what appears to be original blue. Action is tight and retains 90% original case color, silvering on beads, and sharp edges, fading slightly on bottom. Lockplates retain virtually all their original case hardening color and lacquer. Between 1950 and 2000 Purdey's produced fewer than 450 Woodward designed O-U's, an average of 9 per year. This is a fine example in an unusual configuration. **$51,750**

Savage Model 1899 Rifle Factory Engraved

This Model 1899, SN 33302, .303 caliber, represents one of the finest factory engraved rifles ever made. Receiver is engraved in D grade patterns, referred to as the rival grade, with full matted background. On the bottom of receiver there is a well executed motif of male moose; oval on left hand side features American Bison with tiger in oval on opposite side. Entire receiver is engraved and matted as well as trigger guard and lever. Buttplate is also matted. Gun has a 26" half octagon barrel, all original sights including tang sight. Very fancy Circassian walnut stock is deeply carved in relief grape vine scroll work on both forearms, side panels and pistol grip area, very much like the Monarch style carving featured on Savage's most elaborately done guns. Excellent condition. **$77,625**

ROCK ISLAND AUCTION CO.

Sharps New Model 1863 Rifle

This Sharps New Model 1863 rifle, SN C.39309, was manufactured in 1865. The Ordnance Department purchased a number of Sharps rifles to arm the U.S. Veteran Volunteer Infantry regiments formed in 1865 to serve as an elite infantry corps. The U.S. Veteran Volunteer Infantry regiments were armed with Sharps, Spencer and Henry rifles; as an incentive to enlistment volunteers were allowed to retain their weapons when they were discharged. The Civil War ended before the U.S. Veteran Volunteer Infantry regiments saw action. The rifle has a 1" rib on the underside of the barrel for a saber bayonet, 900-yard R.S. Lawrence patent folding rear sight, Lawrence pellet primer and stock with casehardened patch box. The barrel is blued and the forearm cap, barrel bands, receiver, hammer, lever, patch box and buttplate have a color case hardened finish. The screws, band springs, rear sight base, breechblock and pellet primer have a fiery niter blue finish. The stock and forearm are straight grain black walnut with an oil finish. The top of the barrel is roll-stamped "SHARPS RIFLE/MANUFG. CO./HARTFORD CONN." in three lines ahead of the rear sight. "NEW MODEL 1863" is roll-stamped between the rear sight and the receiver. **$31,625**

Freund "Boss Gun" Sharps Model 1874

Brothers Frank and George Freund of Cheyenne, Wyoming, were two of the most famous gunsmiths of the Wild West. Their work is prized by collectors. ▶

▶ This spectacular Freund rifle, SN 156725, .40-70 caliber Sharps Bottleneck, with 30" tapered, light, octagon to round barrel, features Freund's Patent Rocky Mountain front sight and Freund's rear "New Field Sight". Top flat of the barrel has the Bridgeport address above the rear sight and the "OLD RELIABLE" cartouche back of the rear sight with the caliber marking toward the receiver. Mounted with very highly figured, burl and flame grain, uncheckered American walnut with round, schnable tip Sharps forearm and straight stock with nickel buttplate. It has double set triggers. Receiver is engraved in relief with "FREUND IMPROV'D" on left side and rear flat and the Freund name and "PATENTED" with two patent dates on left front flat. Right side is relief engraved "AMERICAN FRONTIER". Lockplate is engraved in script "Freund and Bros Cheyenne W.T. U.S. of A." The area behind the loading slot is engraved in foliate arabesque patterns surrounding "BOSS / GUN". This extraordinary rifle is considered by Sharps collectors to be one of the finest of its type existing today. **$166,750**

Sharps Model 1874 Heavy Buffalo Rifle With Original Scope

This is an extraordinarily rare Model 1874 heavy buffalo rifle with scope, SN C53900, .44-77 Sharps. The rifle has a 30" heavy octagon barrel mounted with a rare "SHARPS" marked full length 34-1/2" telescope that has very fine spider web cross hairs and a brass eye piece aperture. Scope is marked "SHARPS RIFLE MANUFG CO HARTFORD CONN". It has double set triggers and is mounted with very nicely figured, uncheckered American walnut with standard round Sharps forearm that has pewter tip and a straight stock with smooth steel buttplate. Accompanied by its original leather case (48-1/2" x 7-3/4" x 3-1/2"). Also accompanied by a Sharps letter stating the gun was invoiced Aug. 3, 1874 to Schuyler, Hartley and Graham. ▶

CAP. AWL

▶ The rifle was once owned by Jay Gould, one of the world's wealthiest men and railroad magnates. Gould reportedly bought it to try his hand at buffalo hunting. The story goes that he and several friends had a flat car attached to a private train and headed west. When Gould fired this rifle the first time it kicked him off the rail car. He never fired it again, returning it to its case and back to New York. The rifle, in its case, was allegedly discovered in 1946 in the attic of the Gould Foundation School in Spring Valley, New York. Barrel retains 98-99% strong original blue. **$103,500**

Sharps Buffalo Hunter's Rifle and Gear

$86,250

"Sharps Rifle" was often synonymous with "Buffalo Rifle" in Western lore. Although other makers were used, such as Remington, Sharps rifles were most widely selected by professional buffalo hunters during the height of the era (1867-1882). Weighing in at 12-1/2 pounds, this rare Sharps Sporting Rifle, SN C52981, .50-70-caliber, with 30" octagon barrel, is a wonderful example of a buffalo hunter's choice of weapon. The rear sight is an original Lawrence Patent ladder sight and it has an original sporting windgauge tang sight with 3-5/8" staff without graduations. Mounted with uncheckered, highly figured, center crotch American walnut with pewter tipped Sharps forearm and straight stock with smooth Sharps steel buttplate. It has double set triggers. Along with the rifle is an authentic oak and mahogany custom transport case; an original Sharps .50-caliber mold with sprue cutter; a Hall rifle .50-caliber nutcracker ball mold; an original box of ten Sharps Rifle Co. .50-caliber cartridges; an empty du Pont FFG Indian Rifle gun powder tin; an H. Boker brass and iron buffalo hide scale; a leather cartridge

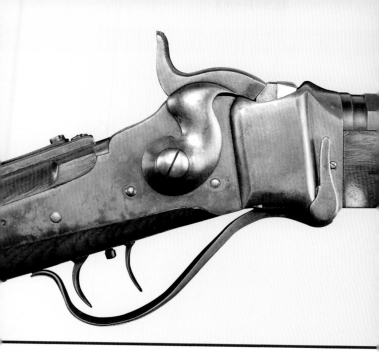

belt with shoulder harness and 32 sewn-on cartridge loops for large cartridges; 24 .50-70-caliber cartridges; a pair of buffalo hide gauntlets; and a Russell Green River skinning knife. This is a wonderful and probably complete buffalo hunter's kit from the 1870s rarely encountered today. **$86,250**

Sharps Model 1874 Sporting Rifle

The Sharps Model 1874 Rifle was manufactured by the Sharps Rife Manufacturing Co., Hartford, Conn., 1871-1881. The name "Model 1874" was not applied to the rifle until a few years after production began. The Model 1874 offers a great variety of features, calibers, barrel lengths, weights, finishes, stocks, buttplates and sights. This example, SN 156339, .44-47-caliber, is a standard sporting rifle with 34" octagon barrel, adjustable globe front sight and no provision for a rear sight. Top flat of barrel has the Sharps Bridgeport address and "CALIBRE 44" over chamber. Receiver has the Sharps name and patent number on the left side and is mounted with a Vernier tang sight with 5" staff matching numbered to this rifle. Rifle is also mounted with uncheckered straight grain American walnut with semi-schnable tip forearm and straight stock with Sharps smooth steel buttplate. Barrel channel also has the full SN in pencil along with the stamped name "C.W. LENNOX". According to Sharps Firearms, there were 3,881 sporting rifles produced at Bridgeport during the period 1871-1880. **$17,250**

PHOTO COURTESY JAMES D. JULIA, INC.

Sharps-Borchardt Model 1878 Rifle

Developed by Hugo Borchardt, who became more famous in later years for his automatic pistol as well as the basic design for the Luger pistol, the Model 1878 was made by Sharps Rifle Co., Bridgeport, Conn., from 1878-1881. A total of 8,700 rifles were produced. This long-range, single-shot rifle, SN 328 .45-caliber, chambered for 2-4/10" case length, has a 34" heavy, tapered round barrel with spirit level wind gauge globe front sight that has the spirit level broken and top of sight slightly mashed with no rear seat. Top of barrel has the "OLD RELIABLE" marking and Bridgeport address. Receiver is color case hardened with integral tang sight base in top tang that contains a 5" Vernier staff with a corresponding heel mount on top of stock. Receiver has inlaid walnut panels on each side. Mounted with nicely figured checkered English walnut. The rifle originally sold for $125. **$15,340**

Smith & Wesson 320 Revolving Rifle

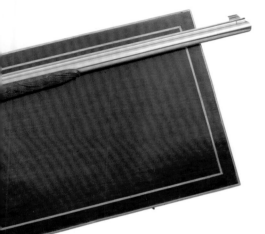

Introduced 1879 and manufactured until 1887, only 977 Revolving Rifles were produced, making it one of the most rare Smith & Wesson firearms produced. Somewhat of a novelty of its time, the idea behind the rifle was that it was easy to conceal, quick to assemble, could fire a long cartridge accurate up to 300 yards and powerful enough to take down a deer. ▶

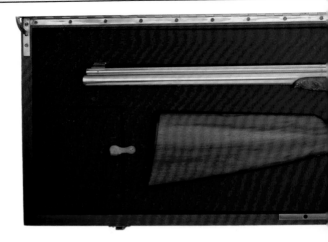

▶ Serial numbered from 1 to 977, the Model 320 was manufactured using the frame and basic action of the New Model No. 3 revolver with some minor differences in the hammer, cylinder and trigger. A slot is cut into the butt and a hole drilled in the back strap to accommodate the shoulder stock. Only 7% of all 320 revolving rifles were nickel-plated. The rifle features an 18" barrel with an interchangeable front blade sight and two leaf folding rear sight. The rifle is chambered for the 320 S&W cartridge invented specifically for this rifle. The top of the rib is marked with the two line address/

patent dates. The matching serial number appears on the butt, cylinder and barrel latch. The barrel is fitted with a checkered mottled red hard rubber forearm with the S&W monogram. The stock is smooth Circassian walnut with nickel finished attaching iron and a checkered black hard rubber buttplate with S&W monogram. Accompanied by an impressive deluxe walnut presentation case. The center lid of the case features a large silver presentation plaque bearing the initials "N.F." The lid of the case features a German silver double border. The interior is blue velvet lined with a cartridge compartment. **$97,750**

Smith & Wesson Model 320 Revolving Rifle

DIRECTIONS FOR USING
Smith & Wesson's Revolving Rifle Reloading Tools.

To remove the exploded caps: Place the head of the shell in the hole on the base, and force the cap out with the wooden punch.

To recap the shells: Place the shell in the hole on one side of the mould, (with the head inside,) place the cap in the orifice of the head, and press it home by the handles of the mould.

To charge the shell: Press it in the Reloader (at the large end,) place it on the base with its head in the countersink; put in powder with small measure, using no more than (but measure full,) place the bullet in the Reloader, ball down, and drive it home with the plunger, until the ____ lar of the plunger strikes the Reloader, (using the ____ mallet.)

To grease the cartridges: Dip the bullets, up to the shells, in melted beef tallow.

This scarce and rare Model 320, SN 522, 320 S&W rifle caliber, six-shot fluted cylinder. The Model 320 was constructed using the frame, cylinder and basic action of the New Model No. 3 Revolver. Accompanied by an original attachable buttstock that has S&W embossed hard rubber buttplate. Yoke of the stock is blued steel with a threaded recess in the top tang for an attachable lollipop peep sight. Accompanied by a Smith & Wesson factory letter indicating this gun being shipped with an 18" barrel, blue finish, mottled hard rubber grips and forend on 10-15-1883 to M.W. Robinson, New York, NY who was S&W's largest distributor. The shipment was for ten units at a cost of $20.50 each. **$63,250**

PHOTO COURTESY JAMES D. JULIA, INC.

Stevens M-520 Trench Shotgun

This Stevens Model 520 shotgun, SN 60103A, .12-gauge, 20" barrel, comes complete with bayonet lug and perforated metal barrel guard. Semi-pistol grip stock, with 11-ring wooden pump actuator and sling swivels. Action operates smoothly and properly; this weapon appears fully functional. This is a very fine example of a trench shotgun. **$6,900**

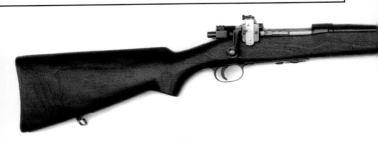

A superb example of a completely original Springfield Model 1922 M1 bolt-action rifle, SN 19633, made from 1924 through 1933. The top of the receiver ring is marked "U.S./ SPRINGFIELD/ ARMORY/ M1922 / MI. CAL..22" over serial number. The rifle has a Lyman 48C micrometer rear sight and a raised ramp front sight, with the top of the barrel and receiver ring drilled and tapped by the factory. Mounted with a one piece smooth American black walnut pistol grip stock with checkered steel buttplate. Accompanied by correct magazine. CONDITION: Extremely fine. **$2,070**

Custer's Model 1865 Spencer Carbine

This Gen. George Armstrong Custer Army-Issue Model 1865 Spencer Carbine was once part of the legendary collection of Dr. Lawrence A. Frost of Monroe, Mich., who had what may have been the most extensive private collection of Custer artifacts and relics assembled. A signed identification tag in Frost's hand accompanies the gun identifies it as a "Spencer Carbine - Saddle Ring / Cal. 50, No. 3658, Model 1865 / 'G. Custer - 7 Cav USA' cut into wooden stock...Used by Gen. Custer in Kansas in 1867 campaign." Custer used a wide range of military and commercially available firearms over the course of his career, but he had a special familiarity with Spencer carbines. Custer's regard for his Spencer carbine is noted in his autobiography, "My Life on the Plains," where he writes: "Leaping from my bed I grasped my trusty Spencer which was always at my side." His Spencer shows

an even patina of honest use. The metal portions are an even gray, with slight salt and peppering, and a few very minor small dents mentioned for accuracy. The wood is in good shape and has not been refinished, with several old dents and a small piece missing where the forestock meets the receiver. The carved inscription clearly shows wear and patina consistent with the rest of the stock. Original saddle ring present, part of front sight missing. The action is crisp and tight, the bore excellent. **$179,250**

Custer's Personal Gun Belt with Holster

This gun belt used by Gen. George Armstrong Custer was once part of the private collection of Dr. Lawrence A. Frost of Monroe, Mich. Custer appears to be wearing this holster in two photographs on horseback taken by Timothy O'Sullivan in June 1863. The holster has a distinct rounded "notch" toward the back of the flap. Such a "notch" is clearly visible on the holster worn by Custer in the two 1863 photos. While showing obvious wear from use, the belt and attachments are in very good condition. All elements have similar patina and have been assembled this way since Civil War times. Overall length is 31-½" including buckle. **$71,700**

Custer Leading 7th Cavalry

Original oil painting (18-1/2" x 24-1/2") by Frederic Remington showing Gen. George Armstrong Custer leading the 7th Cavalry at the Battle of Washita during the Southern Plains Indian Wars. Remington painted this work 20 years after the battle on Nov. 27, 1868, to illustrate Edward Eggelston's book "The Household History of the United States and its People", when it was still regarded as a historically important conflict. **$179,250**

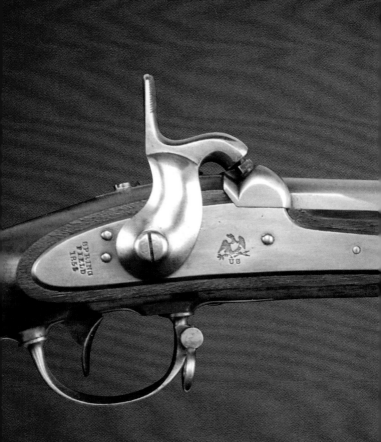

SPRING
FIELD
1856

US

Springfield Model 1842 Musket

This is a single-shot muzzleloader chambered for .69-caliber percussion. It has a 42" round barrel and a full-length stock held on by three barrel bands. There were approximately 275,000 Model 1842 muskets manufactured between 1844 and 1855 by both the Springfield Armory and the Harper's Ferry Armory. This musket, SN NSN, has standard configuration and markings. "1853" dated barrel and lock. "JAS" inspector initials are on left side. CONDITION: Excellent. **$8,625**

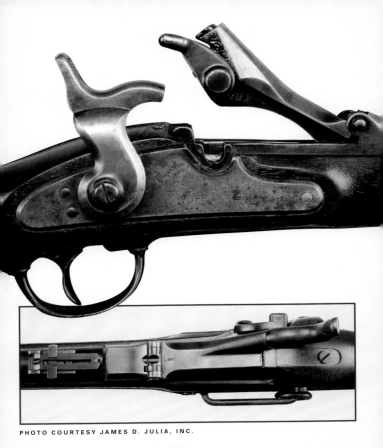

Springfield Model 1870 Saddle Ring Carbine

Springfield Armory produced only 362 of these experimental carbines between April and December 1871. This .50 caliber is probably from the last 20 produced in November 1871 for sale to officers at San Antonio arsenal. The model 1870 was developed from the model 1868 in an attempt to reduce weight. The receiver was shortened and the breechblock considerably lightened. This particular carbine conforms to the normal late run with its 22" round barrel with brass blade front sight, "1870" eagle head and U. S. marked low profile, but high arch, breechblock, saddle ring on long bar on left side, and typical model 1863 lock and stock furniture. CONDITION: Very Fine. **$12,650**

Springfield Model 1875 U.S. "Trapdoor" Officer's Model

The Officer's Rifle, made from 1875-1885, was not issued but was sold to Army officers for personal sporting use.

PHOTO COURTESY JAMES D. JULIA, INC.

One of the attractions of service in the American West was the excellent hunting and this model offered a quality rifle chambered for the standard military cartridge. Only 477 were manufactured but the rifles are not serial numbered. This fine example is nicely finished and has 26" round barrel with 1873 rear sight and Beech combination front. Case hardened receiver has 1873 dated high arch breechblock. Case hardened lock is marked "U. S. Springfield 1873". Breech, lock, hammer, trigger guard, buttplate, and nosecap, are engraved with nicely cut open scroll with acanthus highlights. Rifle is furnished with set trigger, rounded pewter engraved forend tip, and hickory cleaning rod with nickel-plated tip. Barrel retains 90 - 95% original blue, silvering at muzzle, and thinning somewhat overall. CONDITION: Excellent. **$26,450**

Thompson Model 1928 Submachine Gun

A really great condition Thompson, SN 2807A. .45 caliber, 12-1/2" barrel with compensator, Thompson marked Cutts compensator (4 slot). Vertical forend, flip-up rear ladder-type sight adjustable to 600 yards. West Hurley, New York Manufacture select fire. Rear sling swivel on bottom of stock. Includes one 30 round magazine. BATFE has classified this as a Curio and Relic. The firing mechanism fires smoothly when fired by hand, this weapon appears fully functional. CONDITION: Overall finish and appearance, near new except for one vertical crack down right hand side of grip, and a couple of dings to the buttstock. Deep lustrous blue on all metal surfaces is excellent, near 100%. **$16,100**

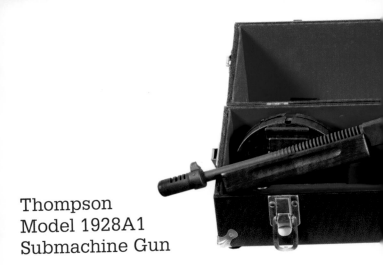

Thompson
Model 1928A1
Submachine Gun

This is a very fine example of a Model 1928A1 Thompson Submachine Gun, as produced by the Savage Arms Corp. These Thompson SMGs were the quintessential classic submachine guns used by early FBI, law enforcement agencies and the military in the late 1920s, throughout WWII, Korea and even into Vietnam. This particular submachine gun is a very late Model 1928A1 SMG as manufactured under a US Army contract by the Savage Arms Corp.

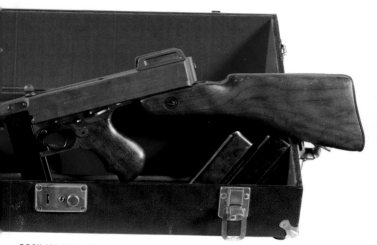

This example still retains some of the earlier and desirable features such as the short 10-1/2" finned barrel with Auto Ordnance Cutts compensator; the detachable butt stock; and the fully adjustable Lyman tangent rear sight with ear protectors. The gun is complete with three 20-round stick magazines, a Seymour Products Company and one Auto Ordnance Company, a Kerr No-Buckle canvas sling and a Thompson marked 50-round drum magazines. **$25,875**

Thompson Model 1928 A22-.22LR Submachine Gun

This West Hurley-manufactured .22-caliber Thompson, SN 244TF, 12-1/2" barrel with Thompson marked Cutts compensator, is presented as new in box with three magazines, mag-well adapter, original brochure and paperwork as provided by Auto Ordnance Corp. in the early 1980s. Only about 100 of these neat little guns were ever produced and registered. Appears new in the box and the condition supports this. Firing mechanism functions smoothly when operated by hand. This weapon appears fully functional. CONDITION: Overall finish and appearance is as new in box. There is evidence of the bolt going back and forth particularly on the face of the chamber where there is some wear. The bolt has a tendency to bounce off of the face of the chamber but this may be normal for this arm. Condition appears unfired. No blemishes to the finish, stock or wood. **$20,700**

Thompson WWII M1A1 Submachine Gun

This is an excellent example of an original WWII Thompson M1A1 Submachine Gun (SMG) introduced in April 1942. The M1A1 was simplified production version of the original Model 1928 Thompson SMG, intended for wartime production, making it easier and cheaper to manufacture. This version eliminated the barrel cooling fins, Cutt's compensator, adjustable rear sight and removable butt stock found on the earlier pre-war models. It has a fixed rear sight, horizontal forearm, fixed butt stock and side-mounted cocking handle. The left side of the receiver is marked "THOMPSON SUBMACHINE GUN/CALIBER 45 M1/A1/NO. 432620" in three lines below the rear sight. The right rear of the receiver is marked "AUTO ORDNANCE CORPORATION/BRIDGEPORT CONNECTICUT U.S.A." in two lines. "US PROPERTY" is stamped on the top rear of the receiver behind the rear sight protector. This SMG is complete with 5 green canvas magazine pouches, with 13 magazines total, a green canvas sling and green canvas carrying case. Included with the rifle is a WWII era U.S. manual. **$25,875**

Thompson
Submachine
Gun

ROCK ISLAND AUCTION CO.

A beautiful example of an exceptional all original transferable Colt Auto Ordnance Thompson 1921/1928 US Navy over-stamp submachine gun. This submachine gun was originally produced in the 1921 configuration, and later over-stamped with "U.S. NAVY MODEL OF 1928". This series of SMGs are still probably the best machined and hand fitted SMGs ever produced. This weapon, SN 8689, still has all the traditional and distinctive features found on these early 1921/28 models so easily recognizable in the Gangster and WWII movies. These features are: 1) the Auto Ordnance ported compensator on the end of the barrel, 2) the short 10-1/2" barrel with cooling fins, 3) the vertical pistol grip, 4) the detachable buttstock, and 5) the fully adjustable Thompson ladder rear sight that is graduated from 100-600 yards. **$37,375**

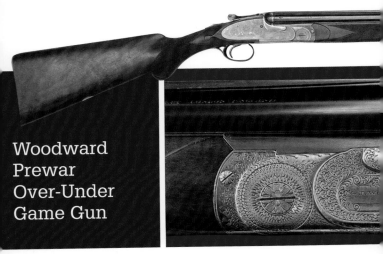

Woodward Prewar Over-Under Game Gun

Prior to World War II, James Woodward & Sons produced a variety of boxlock and sidelock shotguns that are regarded as some of the best made. This .20 gauge over-under, SN 6950, (1931) has 28" Demi-bloc barrels with solid, matted rib fitted with red beads, and are engraved "James Woodward and Sons on left side of top barrel. Scaled down, beautifully sculpted, case hardened, low profile, sidelock action features automatic safety (SAFE inlaid in gold) with Woodward's typical

T-shaped safety slide, reinforcing bolsters, gold band tumbler end cocking indicators, and Boss single non-selective trigger (trigger plate engraved "Boss's Patent No 22894"). The Boss trigger was the finest of its kind and coveted by London makers. **$43,700**

Woodward Best Sidelock Over-Under Pigeon Gun

Exceptionally fine and rare shotgun, SN 6798 (1927), .12 gauge, 2-3/4" Chambers with 30" Demi-bloc barrels mounted with matted, flat, ventilated rib fitted with two red target beads, are engraved "James Woodward and Sons. 64. St. James's Street. London. England." on left side of top barrel. Robust, case hardened, deeply filed detonating, low profile action features automatic "T-safety" (SAFE inlaid in gold), double triggers, and gold line tumbler end cocking indicators. Action and lockplates are engraved in superb Woodward style with very finely cut small scrollwork with rose bouquet highlights. "J. Woodward and Sons" is roll scroll flanked at front of each lockplate. **$41,400**

UMC Cartridge Board

Wonderful UMC cartridge board in its original varnished oak frame (54-1/2" x 41-1/2") with cast plaster panels at top and bottom that read "TRADE U.M.C. MARK" on the top and "THE UNION METALLIC CARTRIDGE CO." on the bottom. Frame is 4" wide varnished oak with glass front and an inner frame of silver plated gesso. The display includes 36 rimfire cartridges, three pinfire cartridges, 126 centerfire cartridges, seven paper shot shells, nine brass shot shells including two cut-aways, nine shot shell brass heads, a 1" Gatling round, 20 grooved and paper patch bullets, three blasting caps, three fuses and a small rectangular display in the bottom containing 14 different kinds of caps and primers, four kinds of shotgun wads and overshot cards, all surrounding a diamond shaped vignette in the center depicting a forest scene with three bugling bull elk, two mule deer does and a roebuck, overprinted with large "U.M.C." **$20,700**

UMC Cartridges Advertising Sign

This large tin UMC Cartridges Bull's Eye advertising sign measure 26-1/2" x 18-1/2" and reads: SHOOTING GALLERY - HIT THE BULL'S EYE WITH UMC CARTRIDGES. Sign is in the shape of a bull's head with a drilled lip for mounting. Made by American Art Sign Co., Brooklyn N.Y. Condition: Fair. There is extensive damage to finish on each side. Nicks and dings along the edges and a slight bend to the left horn. **$1,792**

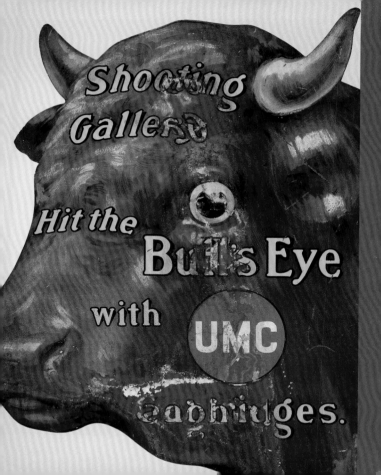

Original Polychrome Remington
UMC Cloth Advertising Banner

The colorful commercial Remington/UMC ammunition fabric advertising banner, depicting mounted Indian warriors hunting buffalo from horseback. Large printed legend reading: Remington/UMC/Arms and Ammunition. Brass grommets in corners for hanging. Size: 27" x 53". **$2,530**

TOP COLLECTOR GUIDES
FOR ANY HOBBYIST

KrauseBooks.com is your one-stop shop for all of your hobby and collecting needs. Whether you are just getting started or have been collecting for years, our products will help you build, identify, appraise and maintain your collections.

You'll find great products at great prices throughout the site and we even offer **FREE Shipping** on purchases over $49.

Be sure to sign up for to receive exclusive offers and discounts!

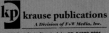
krause publications
A Division of F+W Media, Inc.
700 East State Street • Iola, WI 54990-0001

Antique Trader®
www.antiquetrader.com